THE RECREATION CENTER
OPERATION MANUAL

THE
RECREATION

Alan R. Caskey

CENTER OPERATION MANUAL

SOUTH BRUNSWICK AND NEW YORK:
A. S. BARNES AND COMPANY
LONDON: THOMAS YOSELOFF LTD

© 1972 by A. S. Barnes and Co., Inc.

A. S. Barnes and Co., Inc.
Cranbury, New Jersey 08512

Thomas Yoseloff Ltd
108 New Bond Street
London W1Y OQX, England

Library of Congress Cataloging in Publication Data

Caskey, Alan R
The recreation center operation manual.

Bibliography: p.
1. Recreation centers.   I. Title.
GV182.C37   658'.91'790068   75-146749
ISBN 0-498-07793-4 ·

Printed in the United States of America

To
Dr. Allen V. Sapora
Master Teacher
this manual is
respectfully dedicated

CONTENTS

FOREWORD

This manual consists mainly of material from actual recreation center operating manuals. Almost all data are for an actual recreation center, but in developing your specific center manual, you can adapt this information to suit your own needs. My "helpful hints" recommending how to apply the procedures listed in the manual are in italics, in a manner similar to this Foreword.

This manual emphasizes center administrative and maintenance procedures. Detailed recreation programming information would be too lengthy to be included, and is readily available in other sources.

Recreation centers' functions are changing drastically. The multi-purpose separate building community center is being supplemented by the special recreation facility and the combined school-community recreation concept. This manual reflects some of this change. Special recreation facilities (i.e., artificial ice rinks, swimming pools, tennis buildings) operating procedures are separate manual topics.

This manual does not have all the solutions to your problems as a recreation center director. However, I hope it solves some of your administrative and maintenance problems so that you can concentrate your efforts on creative leadership.

PREFACE

ADMINISTRATION OF RECREATION CENTERS

The leisure time interests of a city's children, teenagers, and adults are many. In an effort to provide recreation opportunities for all ages, the overall program must involve activities in the areas of athletics and sports, music, drama, dancing, arts and crafts, social recreation, etc. The promotion, organization, and conduct of such activities pose many problems. One of the very important factors in a successful operation is organizing the department so that it will function as efficiently and economically as possible.

As a large number of employees work only on a part-time basis it becomes necessary for the limited number of full-time employees to participate in the planning and evaluating of programs, in the conducting of activities, and in the carrying out of certain administrative assignments. Responsibilities must be delegated, duties clearly defined, and the limits of authority prescribed at each level of position. The principle of direct relationship must prevail with the line of communication definitely understood.

For this reason, a recreation center staff needs to have a manual of procedure. It is hoped that this manual will serve as a tool for good administration of a recreation center.

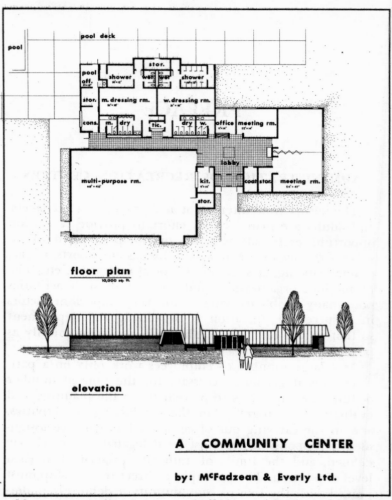

floor plan
10,000 sq. ft.

elevation

A COMMUNITY CENTER

by: McFadzean & Everly Ltd.

Many community centers are built in conjunction with other recreation facilities. This neighborhood center is built in conjunction with a swimming pool.

OBJECTIVE OF RECREATION CENTER PROGRAM

The primary objective of a recreation center program is to provide a variety of activities to help individuals gain the greatest satisfaction and benefit from their leisure.

SPECIAL ACKNOWLEDGMENTS

Special thanks is extended to the city, state, and federal recreation agencies whose recreation center operation manuals and other material has been used in this manual.

Topeka, Kansas	New York State
Rockford, Illinois	New Jersey State
Milwaukee, Wisconsin	United States Army
Evanston, Illinois	McFadzean and Everly, LTD.

SPECIAL ACKNOWLEDGMENTS

THE RECREATION CENTER
OPERATION MANUAL

1

INTRODUCTION

PLANNING THE RECREATION CENTER

Recreation centers should be functionally designed to provide a program consistent with their size and suitable to the community they serve. In every instance, the planning should provide for flexibility in use and for future expansion.

Functional Planning

In considering the recreation needs of any municipality, a comprehensive master plan should be prepared that coordinates anticipated future development and expansion of school and other public recreation resources with the best possible use of existing facilities. To obtain the best results in functional planning, close cooperation between the school and recreation authorities, municipal planning boards, and architects is essential. In addition, it is necessary that the actual construction be repeatedly checked to assure that the facilities are constructed according to specifications. It should be clearly understood that all of these specific plans and recommendations are subject to variations and conditions of local situations.

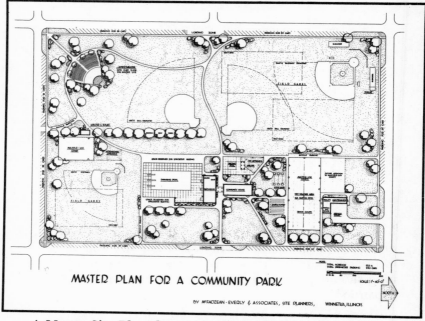

MASTER PLAN FOR A COMMUNITY PARK

BY McFADZEAN · EVERLY & ASSOCIATES, SITE PLANNERS,   WINNETKA, ILLINOIS

A Master Site Plan shows the relationship between a recreation center and other park facilities.

In planning recreation centers, consideration should be given to their relation to existing and potential outdoor facilities. Long-term planning should be in broad general terms. Immediate planning should be detailed—meeting immediate needs—and should be supplementary to and in accordance with the master plan, as well as be related to future needs for buildings designed for specific activities, and for multiple-use facilities to satisfy the recreational needs of the entire community.

Plotting the course and the design and construction of such indoor recreation facilities should begin with the local recreation agency and the recreation administrator.

This course should be dictated not by personal opinion or preference, but by past experience in the evaluation of public acceptance of such projects, the clearly indicated interest and desire on the part of people to be served, and their expressed willingness to share in the problems of design, construction, operation, and cost.

Determining Needs and Establishing Priorities

The next step is to explore the needs of the various neighborhoods of the community to be serviced by this project. Since it is seldom possible to satisfy the wants of any community with one single project, it is well to set up a list of priorities. The safest rule to follow is to establish priorities on the basic concept of *"the greatest good for the greatest number."* If local recreation commissions adhere to this rule, their program will be sound and will have general acceptance by the entire populace of the community.

Having determined the order of priority, the next step is to prepare a general floor plan, determine in rough general terms the cost, and prepare colorful renderings of the proposed construction. This material should be presented to the appropriating authorities by the local recreation commission. Specific details can be discussed and general agreement reached on the methods of financing, and at least a rough estimate of the cost of the entire program.

Plans should then be revised in terms of procedures outlined above, and detailed drawings and more accurate cost estimates should be prepared in the light of the altered plans. All building plans should be approved by the appropriate regulating authority of the municipality.

Financing the Project

Generally, municipal recreation buildings are constructed and operated by municipal tax funds. These funds are provided for by the local appropriating authority to the local recreation department. These buildings are open for use by the public without charge, and in most instances no attempt is made to help meet the actual cost of construction or operation by charging admission or by use of rental fees.

Items in the operating budget of a recreation center are:

1. Salaries and wages of leadership and maintenance personnel
2. Fuel
3. Light
4. Water
5. Recreation and office supplies
6. Janitorial supplies
7. Repairs and miscellaneous expense

Types of Recreation Centers

COMMUNITY RECREATION CENTER (LARGE)

The Community Recreation Center (Large) is functionally designed and planned to make possible a varied program of recreation activities for all age groups. These activities may be social, creative, cultural, or physical in nature. The building should provide a safe, healthful, and attractive atmosphere in which children and adults may enjoy their leisure.

Area to be served. This building serves a geographical area in which the school facilities are inadequate, or unavailable. It is designed for use on a neighborhood park or playground and should be located so as to serve the greatest number of persons within a mile radius, depending upon local conditions and the density of population.

Size. It is suggested that the building contain approxi-

A recreation center should be located as close as possible to the center of the area it serves. However, because of present housing patterns, recreation centers might have to be located at the edge of a service area.

mately 20,000 square feet of floor space.

Assembly Hall. The area of this room should be approximately 4000 square feet. It should be rectangular in shape, with a minimum width of 50 feet. The minimum ceiling height should be 20 feet. The stage proper should be about 20 feet from front to back, and the proscenium opening should be at least two-thirds the width of the room. Dressing rooms, equipped with washbowls and mirrors, should be easily accessible to the stage.

The assembly hall should be designed for multiple use. It should accommodate such activities as general meetings, social recreation, active table games, dancing, dramatics, orchestral practice, concerts, and banquets.

Gymnasium. The over-all size of the gymnasium should be at least 65′ x 90′, with a minimum height of 22′. This size permits a basketball playing court of 42′ x 74′. These dimensions will permit seven tiers of bleachers on one side of the gymnasium, seating approximately 325 spectators. It is well to make sure that bleachers are properly installed and are of an approved type. It is also advisable that the wall plans include recessed housing for these bleachers when closed. The playing court should in no case be closer than six feet to any wall or obstruction.

By the use of folding walls, this gym can be divided into two recreation activity areas.

Dressing–Locker Room. A room for the purpose of changing clothes is necessary and should be in close proximity to the gymnasium. There are two accepted plans for checking personal wearing apparel: (1) locker rooms with metal lockers, and (2) dressing rooms with checkroom for checking clothing in wire baskets.

NOTE: If there is a possibility of a swimming pool being constructed on this site, at some future time, the dressing rooms should be so located and arranged as to serve efficiently both gymnasium and the pool.

Shower Rooms. The size of the shower rooms is dependent upon the extent of the facilities and the largest number of persons to be served efficiently at once. Adequate shower rooms for each sex should be a primary consideration.

Clubrooms. To meet special needs, it is desirable to have two clubrooms. At least one clubroom should be equipped for handicraft use.

Kitchen. The Pullman or unit type of kitchen is recommended. It should be located near the clubrooms. If it is planned to serve large dinners or banquets, provisions should be made for a full-size modern kitchen.

Checkroom. The size of the checkroom will depend on the magnitude of the program. It should open into the lobby of the building. It should be equipped with shelves and portable hanger racks.

Office–First Aid Room. The Office–First Aid Room is the nerve center of the building. It should be located, if possible, adjacent to the lobby, corridor, and clubrooms. The walls should have glass windows to enable the maximum amount of supervision.

Rest Rooms. Rest Rooms for each sex should be provided at each floor level.

COMMUNITY RECREATION CENTER (SMALL)

In some cases, due to existing facilities or limited funds, it will be more appropriate to restrict the size of the community recreation center to approximately 10,000 square feet. In all cases the building should be designed so that rooms can be easily added.

In a building of this size, the facilities may include the following:

1. Gymnasium-social hall-auditorium (or what is sometimes termed "Multi-purpose Room") 60′ x 90′.
2. Lobby-lounge 30′ x 40′ with provisions for food and light beverage dispensing machines.
*3. Office with storage space 10′ x 10′ centrally located.
4. Two rest rooms 8′ x 14′.
5. Two clubrooms 25′ x 30′ each separated by a folding door.

---

* Office can also serve as first aid room.

6. Gymnasium and maintenance storage room 10′ x 12′.

The compact design of this recreation center is necessitated by the small park size.

PLAYGROUND-SHELTER TYPE OF COMMUNITY RECREATION CENTER

The Playground-Shelter Type of Community Recreation Center is a facility to provide opportunities for informal participation, group meeting, and such supervised activities as social recreation, dance instruction, table games, handicraft, art, and music. It may serve as a playground and become the focal point for all recreation activities of that particular neighborhood.

Size. Common practice suggests approximately 1500

square feet of floor space for this type of indoor recreation facility.

Activities Room. The activities room should have a minimum area of 1000 square feet. It is designed to serve as a recreation facility for a variety of informal games, group meetings, and creative activities.

Porch. The porch area should be free from obstruction and provided with lighting. The floor surface should be level and smooth to permit the playing of table games and other activities requiring a level surface.

The three indoor recreation centers described above are but a few of the many types which can be adapted into the over-all community recreation program. The type that will service your community best will be resolved when a survey has been made and a master plan has been put into effect.

Adapting School Buildings for Community Center Programming

POLICY RELATIONSHIPS BETWEEN SCHOOL BOARD AND RECREATION DEPARTMENT

The Recreation Department, as a unit in the municipal government, is brought into close touch with many other departments and must rely on them for assistance in carrying on many of its services. In some cases the recreation authorities cannot avoid such relationships with these departments; in others they have much to gain by enlisting their cooperation.

Education and recreation are closely interrelated; school properties include many facilities suited to community recreation use. It is therefore essential that there be the closest understanding and cooperation between the two authorities. Fortunately, in many states, much progress has been made in this direction, although in some communities there is little evidence of cooperation between these two groups.

School Center. The term "indoor recreation center" is commonly applied to a building which is not used primarily or exclusively for recreation, but in which recreation activities are regularly provided under leadership for community groups. Indoor recreation centers are sometimes provided in city halls, churches, libraries, and other types of buildings, but most frequently in school buildings. In hundreds of communities within each state, schools are opened for community recreation by the recreation authority. The important place that the school center plays in the recreation life of many communities necessitates special consideration of this type of indoor center. The modern school—with its gymnasiums, auditorium, music room, workshops, stage, library, art room, and other features—is admirably equipped for recreation on a community-wide basis. To use these facilities only a few hours a day and to permit them to be idle during long periods when citizens desire to use them is an unjustifiable economic waste. The fact that a well-located school occupies a focal point in the community or neighborhood is another item in its favor. The general opinion prevails that the school building, supported by tax funds and representing a place where all can meet, affords a logical center for the recreational life of the people of a community.

Types of School Centers. Many and varied are the community uses of school buildings for recreation and the methods under which they are conducted. In some instances local organizations such as scout troops, orchestra, or woman's clubs are permitted to use schoolrooms for their regular meetings; in other groups young men or women use the school gymnasium one evening a week for basketball and other games. These types of recreational activities are regularly carried on at school buildings under the leadership of recreation agencies serving all the people of a community. In some instances the agency provides a diversified program utilizing the facilities in the building, which consequently serve as a genuine neighborhood center; but in others it merely uses one or more facilities to furnish specialized activities for community groups.

School Center Hours. Most school centers are open only two or three evenings a week although in many instances a program is carried on from Monday through Friday. The evening periods are usually from two to four hours in length, although they vary from city to city, and sometimes when a special event such as a dance is held, the center is kept open later than usual. As a rule, the center

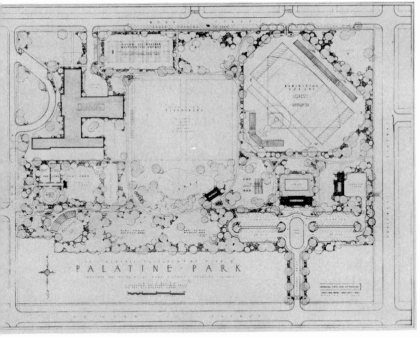

A school can and often is used as the recreation center. Recreation activities are scheduled during non-school hours.

season extends from early in the fall until well into the spring, but if the center is operated in connection with an outdoor play area, the program extends throughout the year.

When preparing a calendar for use of school parcels into the overall recreation of a community it is well to take into consideration this rule: "The school calendar must be fulfilled before scheduling any activities for community-wide usage for recreation."

PARK, SCHOOL AND RECREATION COOPERATION

Schools, parks, and recreation programs result from the American public's desire for educational and recreational facilities and opportunities. Increased urban growth, coupled with increasing population pressures, is leading to intensified demands on public park, recreation, and school agencies for an increasing variety of facilities and services. The need to design and use the facilities of these agencies for the greatest public good is heightened by the heavy demands on tax dollars available for these purposes.

School, recreation, and park authorities throughout the country are exploring ways and means of working co-operatively for mutual advantage and increased service to the communities they serve. Through joint efforts, each agency can contribute to greater public service without giving up its identity or any of its legitimate responsibilities.

It is desirable that a working relationship, as expressed in a written joint agreement, be established before either the park, recreation, or school agency makes extensive use of the other's resources. Failure to establish such a working relationship may result in misuse or misunderstandings concerning the use of the facilities. Unfortunate occurrences of this nature have, in some communities, hindered the provision of programs and services that make the best possible use of public facilities.

A park, school, and recreation agreement should provide a sound arrangement for cooperative planning and action, and should include the following elements:

a. A declaration of intent by all boards concerned to accept cooperative responsibility in the provision of such areas, facilities, and supervision as may be required to meet the recreational needs of the constituency, consistent with the authority granted to each through enabling state legislation;

b. Agreement by the School District that its areas and facilities may be considered available for recreational uses by citizens within such limitations as ·may have to be placed upon their use by reason of the suitability of the area or facility involved, and prior claims of established or planned school activities, or by reason of other logical considerations;

c. Agreement by the Park and Recreation Boards that their areas and facilities may be considered available to the School District under conditions corresponding to those set forth above for the use of school property;

d. In view of the recognition of the cooperative responsibility of the respective boards to render the largest possible recreation service to the citizens of the community, each board should express its willingness to grant the other the use of its facilities and areas generally in preference to non-public agencies, consistent with such rules and exceptions as may be considered necessary and desirable;

e. Land acquisition policies should be set forth with due consideration for location, size, influence area, site design, and development cost. Site acquisition should precede, wherever possible, the urban development of the area it is to serve;

f. Agreement concerning responsibility for area and facility design and development in keeping with the principle that in general the Park Board is better equipped to develop recreation areas and facilities. and the School Districts are better equipped to construct educational facilities;

g. Agreement concerning responsibility for maintenance in keeping with the principle that in general the Park Board is better equipped to maintain outdoor areas and facilities, and the School District is better equipped to maintain its own indoor facilities;

h. Supervision responsibility agreement in keeping with the principle that in general, when one agency uses the other's facility, it shall accept full responsibility for the provision of qualified supervision over the activity and responsibility for any damages resulting

NILES PARK RECREATION CENTER
NILES, ILLINOIS

This recreation center and swimming pool was designed for a community of 20,000 people.

from the use of the facility other than normal wear and tear; and,

i. Cost sharing agreement, which should be determined, whenever possible, on the basis of exchange of services and privileges rather than on the basis of cross-billing for services and privileges.

Allocation of Public School Facilities for Recreation Purposes

The most desirable way to allocate facilities is to establish a policy and to make this policy known to prospective users of the facility. Policy considerations should include the following:

a. A listing of facilities which may be used for recreational purposes;

b. A description of each facility and the purposes for which it is suitable;

c. Rules and regulations governing the use of the facility;

d. Cost for the use of the facility; and,

e. Method of deciding priority of allocation. This should be clearly stated in order to avoid misunderstanding and conflict.

Groups seeking permits for the use of Board of Education, physical education and classroom or auditorium facilities should be recognized on a priority basis such as the one indicated below.

Suggested Priorities for Issuing Permits

1. LOCAL SCHOOLS

Each school should have the full use of its own facilities during the regular school day and until 6:00 P.M. except as noted later in this paragraph. Following this hour, the facility should be considered open for permit requests on a "city-wide" basis, with requests from the local schools being honored first. Each school desiring the evening use of physical education or other facilities should anticipate its needs for one semester in advance. Lists of these anticipated needs should be sent to the central school district office for the first semester by October 1, and for the second semester by January 1. No requests need be made for the school's own facilities before 6.00 p.m. except when it is necessary for that school to share its facilities with another school. Under such conditions, the facilities should be considered as "city-wide."

2. OTHER SCHOOLS

The requests of other schools for recreational activities should be honored ahead of those of outside groups. The lists of the anticipated needs of all schools submitted to the central office should be used in assigning permit times of the various schools to the facilities available.

3. PUBLIC SCHOOL RECREATION ACTIVITIES

In addition to the physical education or the athletic use of school plants by the public schools, schools occasionally wish to schedule other recreational activities. It is understood that small group dances and parties and other recreational activities involving small numbers should be scheduled wherever possible in smaller rooms in order that the main gymnasium rooms may be kept available for those recreation programs requiring the larger space. If, however, a large school dance is to be sponsored for a school having a gymnasium or by a public school wishing to use another school's gymnasium, the larger gymnasium rooms should be made available on a permit basis.

4. RECREATION BOARD

When the needs of the schools (including P.T.A.

Each public recreation building is designed for a specific recreation activity. Converting a gym to a card party area causes additional maintenance tasks.

groups) have been met, the requests of the Recreation Board for facilities for their use in promoting community recreation programs should be recognized first for the remaining time.

5. OTHER RECREATION GROUPS

After the Recreation Department has set up its program of activities in such a manner that time to be consumed in the facility is definite, the requests of other individuals and organizations should be considered, with preference given to requests involving recreational activities.

6. OTHER NON-RECREATIONAL GROUPS

The requests of other miscellaneous community groups and organizations conducting activities not related to recreation should be honored if there is time remaining and the activities are appropriate for the facility requested.

Allocation of Park Facilities for Recreation Purposes

The same policy considerations outlined above should determine the method of allocating and programming Park District facilities. The Recreation Board should be given first priority in programming park facilities, and school requirements should be given preference to other non-public agencies in use of Park District facilities, consistent with such rules and exceptions as may be considered desirable.

Rules and Regulations

The central school district office should prepare the necessary bulletins and application forms to be issued to the various groups seeking permits to use school facilities.

The Park District office should prepare the necessary bulletins and application forms to be issued to the various groups seeking permits to use park facilities, except in those instances where the Recreation Board may be given full programming authorization by the Park District. In such instances, the necessary forms and bulletins should be prepared and issued by the Recreation Board.

2

EMERGENCY PROCEDURES PERTAINING TO CENTER PERSONNEL AND/OR PARTICIPANTS

Protect the health and safety of your center participants. You must know the accident, first aid and emergency procedures before the incident occurs. If an emergency occurs, think—then react. Use your common sense.

ACCIDENT REPORTING

Center personnel will assure that proper procedures are followed in the event of an accident occurring within the confines of their area of responsibility. The following procedures will apply and will be followed after an accident has occurred:

1. Administer first aid, when required, to stop bleeding or relieve pain.
2. In the event of a serious accident, call the police; have the police call an ambulance.
3. Secure transportation for less seriously injured when required.

4. In cases of injuries requiring hospitalization or doctor's care, a follow-up must be made to secure the name of the hospital, the doctor's name, and the diagnosis if possible.

5. Complete the proper accident report form—participant or employee—regardless of type or seriousness of injury. *Fill out every item on the form* (shown in Appendix).

6. Good public relations call for contacting the injured the following day to "find out how he's getting along."

The recreation center director's office area should be close to main access areas.

FIRST AID

A center director will occasionally be called to render treatment to injured persons. The following is a compiled list of suggested procedures to follow in the event of an accident. Do not make the mistake of convincing yourself you are an expert on first aid procedures, but on the other hand, don't hesitate to react in an emergency. It should be noted that you are responsible for first aid—not complete care and treatment.

General Rules

1. Keep injured person lying down, with his head level with the rest of his body unless he has a head injury. In that case, raise his head slightly. Cover the victim and keep him warm.
2. Don't move the injured person except to remove him from fire, flood, smoke, or anything that would further endanger his life.
3. Examine the injured person to determine whether emergency action is necessary. If he is not in danger of bleeding to death, or is not suffocating, or has not been severely burned, or is not in shock, *it is better for the untrained person to leave him alone.*
4. Do not give an unconscious or semi-conscious person anything to drink.
5. Do not let an injured person see his wounds.
6. Reassure him and keep him comfortable.

INJURY	*TREATMENT*
1. Bleeding	Use first aid dressing or clean cloth and apply pressure directly over the wound.

2. Burns — Don't use grease, oil, or ointment. Remove clothing unless it sticks to burn. Cover the burned area with clean dressing or cloth for chemical burns; wash burn thoroughly with water before covering with dressing.

3. Broken Bones — Don't move the area in which the break occurred. It is best to leave the break alone and not splint it. The doctor or ambulance driver will handle this job. If the bone punctures the skin, cover the wound with clean cloth. Apply slight pressure to control bleeding.

4. Shock — Victim may show signs of pale skin, cold skin, rapid pulse, wet with sweat, or unconsciousness. Keep him lying down. Elevate feet slightly. Cover victim with blanket. If he is conscious, give him plenty of water.

5. Cuts — Clean the cut of as much foreign matter as possible. Apply antiseptic to counteract germs. Cover with bandage.

Call the doctor for serious injuries.

Heat Stroke and Heat Exhaustion

Persons subject to: aged, fat, very young, alcoholics, those with illness impairing entire body.

Causes: over exposure to sun or indoor heat.

Prevention: avoid over exposure and over exertion (frequent breaks), increase water and salt intake, lighter clothing and lighter diet.

Symptoms: headache, nausea (vomiting), weakness.

Treatment: remove to cooler place, rest in reclining position (unless detrimental to victim), fluid, no stimulants.

SYMPTOMS

Heat Stroke	*Heat Exhaustion* (1)
Speed up of bodily functions	Slow down of bodily functions
Skin dry-hot	Skin moist-cool
Temperature high	Temperature normal
Rapid-strong pulse	Slow, weak pulse
Redness of face	Paleness of face
Old people more prone to	Age does not contribute
Consciousness lost	Conscious generally
Generally no other symptoms	Abdominal cramps often accompany (2)

TREATMENT

Call a doctor	Call doctor if persists
Cool off slowly by sponging off	Maintain body temperature
Elevate head and upper portion of body (3)	Elevate feet and lower portion of body
Have victim sip salt and soda solution	Have victim sip salt solution
Cold towels on forehead	Warm towels on abdomen for cramps

1. Although causes and symptoms differ, it is interesting to note that some of the treatment for Heat Exhaustion and Shock are very similar.
2. This is one symptom in heat exhaustion which is generally not present in Heat Stroke.
3. This is a reminder of the rhyme often taught in first aid courses. It works so well in many cases that it should be stated: "Color Red, raise the head. Color Pale, raise the tail."
4. Look at the underscored letters under Heat Stroke. If you want to use your imagination and change your spelling to "Konscious, Kall, and Kool," you can see how the letters in Stroke can remind you of most of the symptoms and treatment.
5. Ask to see HEBS—premeasured salt or mixed salt and soda for *H*eat *E*ffects, *B*urns, and *S*hock.

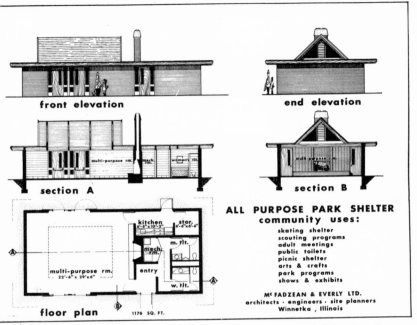

ALL PURPOSE PARK SHELTER
community uses:

skating shelter
scouting programs
adult meetings
public toilets
picnic shelter
arts & crafts
park programs
shows & exhibits

M^cFADZEAN & EVERLY LTD.
architects · engineers · site planners
Winnetka , Illinois

An all-purpose park shelter can serve as a neighborhood recreation center.

Fights

1. Call the park police.
2. Suspend membership.
3. Report incident to immediate supervisor.

Fire Evacuation Procedures

Each center director is responsible for the preparation and posting of a fire evacuation plan to assure the orderly evacuating of the facility in the event of a fire. This plan should be drawn to scale and approved by the local fire marshal. Center personnel will follow the following procedures when a fire—regardless of size—is detected:

1. Evacuate the building in accordance with established and posted plan.
2. Call Fire Department.
3. Use available fire fighting equipment to curtail or eliminate fire.
4. Assist fire department personnel as required.

3

ADMINISTRATIVE FUNCTIONS AND PROCEDURES

REGISTRATION FOR ACTIVITIES

Registration for all youth and young adult activities is accomplished at the same time the participant purchases a membership card. When a new person enters the center, he or she is asked to fill in information on two cards. The membership card remains in the possession of the member; the Rolodex card is placed in a file at the center. The Rolodex file system has proved to be a very simple and efficient method of registration. (See Appendix for Sample Form)

Enrollment in special activities is the responsibility of the specialist. A list of class members, their addresses, and phone numbers should be kept on file at the center. Registrations are sometimes accepted prior to the first class period by the center director.

Eligibility for Membership

All students living in ———— shall be considered eligible for student membership. Student memberships shall be

Recreation centers are providing specialized facilities such as ice skating rinks, swimming pools, and hobby areas.

designated for grade school (grades 1 through 6), junior high (grades 7 through 9), or senior high (grades 10 through 12) general program activities.

Membership Fees

1. The annual student membership fee from September to September shall be: grades 1–6, 50 cents; grades 7–12, $1.00.
2. The replacement fee for student membership cards (grade school) shall be 10 cents. The replacement for all other membership cards shall be 50 cents.
3. There may be fees assessed for special program activities.
4. The fee for young adult membership (ages 19–26) shall be at a rate of $2.00 per membership. This fee may be established when necessary.

NOTE: Membership cards are non-transferrable and non-redeemable.

Membership Privileges

1. Admission to general program activities shall be by membership card only.
2. Admission to special program activities shall be by membership card and fee where applicable.
3. Guests will be admitted upon payment of a fee of 25 cents per session. Guests must be sponsored by a member. The sponsor must be present while the guest is in the center and is responsible for the conduct of his guest.

Combined swimming pool bathhouses and recreation centers provide year-around service.

RULES OF CONDUCT FOR PARTICIPANTS

1. All members who enter the center must sign the membership book. Members leaving evening activities more than 30 minutes before the close of the activity must check their name in the book and enter the time.
2. Food and soft drinks shall be permitted in designated areas only.
3. All equipment shall be used for the purpose for which it was designated.
4. Any member who is disorderly must, upon request, surrender his membership card to the center director or any person duly authorized by him. Further action as to its disposition shall be determined after consultation with the Superintendent of Recreation.
5. Willful destruction of property shall be considered disorderly and subject the offender to dismissal from membership. He, or his legal guardian, shall be liable for the cost of repair and/or replacement.
6. No alcoholic beverages shall be permitted on the premises nor shall any person under the influence of liquor be admitted.
7. No gambling shall be permitted on the premises.
8. Loitering about the entrance or any area surrounding the building is prohibited.
9. Smoking is prohibited unless authorized by the Recreation Commission.

Each center adopts its own rules. You must operate by some guidelines. Make your center enjoyable. Occasionally, and through consultation with your supervisor and Advisory Council, you may want to change or alter a rule.

PROCEDURES FOR DISCIPLINE CASES

Directors or managers of facilities under the jurisdiction

How, then, shall we go about developing a recreation program. The literature in the field of recreation, which in most cases reflects the thinking of professional leaders, offers guiding principles for the organization and conducting of activities. In general, the following broadly interpreted guide for program planning is accepted.

1. Program planning should involve consideration of the diversified recreation interests and desires of the people to be served.
2. Program planning should take into account the age, sex, and economic status of the people to be served.
3. Program participants, paid or volunteer leaders, and governing bodies of the public agency sponsoring the program should share in the process of program planning.
4. Program planning should be related to the physical, mental, social, and emotional characteristics of the people to be served.
5. Program planning should provide an opportunity for participants at varying levels of proficiency and for the instruction in recreation skills.
6. Program planning should provide for the use of all available resources that can provide variety and enrich the program.
7. Program planning should take into consideration the long range plans of the agency for organization, finance, leadership, areas, and facilities.
8. It is policy that social events will not be sponsored to include mixed age groupings, i.e. junior and senior high students. All social events to include mixed age groupings will require approval of the Recreation Commission prior to scheduling.

Instituting New Programs

Center directors will submit to the Superintendent of Recreation requests to begin new programs prior to initiating action to open such programs. Requests will indicate type of program, cost, source of funds, who will direct the activity, reason for the program, and other pertinent information. This procedure will be followed to the letter as new programs may establish precedent and determine policy.

Publicity

1. Radio:
    a. Postcard to program chairman of station three or five days prior to event
    b. State all information about event
2. Newspapers:
    a. Contact newspaper editor, Sunday or daily
    b. State all information
3. Television: Personal contact at station—program chairman
4. School papers: Contact school editor and journalism instructors
5. Posters: Make and distribute
6. Brochures:
    a. Plan brochure
    b. Take to office for mimeographing
7. Adult and Junior Advisory Boards
8. Speeches:
    a. P.T.A.
    b. Mothers study clubs
    c. Optimist clubs
    d. Others

Helpful Hints for Making Your Program Successful

1. Know Community:
    a. Check Bureau of Census
    b. Talk to people:

       i. principals
      ii. residences
     iii. nurses
     iv. ministers
      v. civic associations
     vi. service clubs
    vii. participants
   viii. adult advisory board
  c. Survey community (visual tour)

2. Know Policies Governing Program:
   a. See policy section of manual
   b. Read manual
   c. Consult supervisor
   d. Check written Commission policies and check memos in file

3. Know Other Recreation in Your Neighborhood:
   a. YWCA, YMCA activities
   b. Boy's Club
   c. Clubs
   d. Private recreation (bowling, skating)
   e. Boy Scouts, Girl Scouts
   f. Check school calendars

4. Know Your Facility and Activities:
   a. Share equipment
   b. Know activities that can be programmed

5. Evaluate Previous Programs:
   a. Minutes of Commission meetings
   b. Office and center files
   c. Participants
   d. Evaluate attendance check

6. Plan Basic Program:
   a. Establish goals:
      i. participation
      ii. accomplishments
   b. Establish program:
      i. carry on present program

    ii. make changes
  c. New Program:
      i. talk to other center directors about program
      ii. consultant available through Superintendent
      iii. check periodicals
      iv. determine interest of potential participants in an activity by survey
      v. consult supervisors
      vi. be flexible and plan alternatives
      vii. conduct community attitude survey
7. Special Interest Groups:
  a. Take advantage of groups and clubs that express interest in center.
  b. Publicity—ask for show of interest through papers, television, radio, etc.

EVALUATION OF CENTER PROGRAMS

Quantitative Evaluation

When evaluating the recreation center program, the following points must be considered:
  1. Economic and cultural group in area to be considered.
  2. Types of program—diversified program for all desired interests.
  3. Does scheduling of program meet the needs of the community?
  4. Do the activities bring in the desired attendance?
  5. Are publicity methods adequate?
  6. Does staff show initiative and imagination in programming?
  7. Based upon attendance and the established standards for attendance:

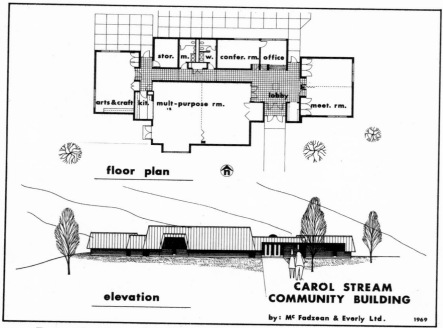

floor plan

elevation

**CAROL STREAM
COMMUNITY BUILDING**

by: Mᶜ Fadzean & Everly Ltd. 1969

Recreation areas should be separated but serviced by a central corridor. This floor plan provides from four to six activity rooms.

   a. Which centers should be discontinued?
   b. Which centers should be operated additional afternoons or evenings?
   c. Which centers should be operated fewer afternoons or evenings?
   d. What activity programs should be expanded?
   e. What activity programs should be discontinued?
   f. How much service was rendered the neighborborhood through permit group meetings?

Sample Center Evaluation

Evening Operation
    Evenings of operation   T-TH
    Total number—For the season   40

    Attendance—Minimum requirement—Per evening   150
    Attendance—Minimum requirement—Season   6000
    Attendance—Total for season—   3972

    Core program—Attendance for season—   2036
    Core program—Average per evening   51
    Core program—Number of different activities offered   4

    Classes—Total attendance—Season—   96
    Other department-sponsored activities—Total
      attendance   1718
    Permit groups—Total attendance   122

Findings—On the basis of the statistical analysis, this center
    should be closed evenings because:

1. The total attendance for the season is 2027 below the minimum requirement.
2. The core program of four activities (teen-age non-membership activities) had an average attendance of 51 per evening, or 13 per activity per evening. The activities offered were basketball, pocket billiards, table tennis, and table games.
3. Only one class materialized and was conducted for 10 evenings with an average attendance of 10 per evening, although 18 enrolled.
4. The Golden Age club and special events accounted for an attendance of 1718, or an average of 44 per week.
5. The use of the center by permit groups was negligible.
6. The center was staffed with a full-time director, two full-time recreation leaders, and several part-time employees.

7. The cost of the full-time staff, the part-time employees, the building engineer, heat, light, water, and telephone was far in excess of the per capita standard for a two-night operation.

Afternoon Operation
Afternoons of operation	5
Total number—For the season	80
Total number—Saturday afternoons	16
Total number of activity sessions—Season	96
Attendance—Minimum requirement—Per session	25
Attendance—Minimum requirement—Season	2000
Attendance—Total for season	2547
Number of different activities offered	10

Findings—One the basis of the statistical analysis, this center should continue its afternoon operation because:

1. The total attendance for the season exceeded the minimum requirement by 3148 and the minimum average per session by 52 (average 162 required 110).
2. All other requirements were met.

Qualitative Evaluation

Based upon conferences with:
1. The center director and his staff
2. The principal of the school
3. The president and the recreation chairmen of the P.T.A.
4. The area supervisor (office staff member)

Findings
1. This center is located in an area subject to racial tensions due to the migration of a new ethnic group to this area.
2. The new residents of this area are in need of recreation services. They are inclined to be slow in availing

themselves of the opportunity offered.

3. The decline in the evening attendance at this center is comparatively recent and has followed the pattern of other centers in which there has been a heavy migration of a new ethnic group.

4. There is not another public recreation center near this area; the center is well located geographically.

5. There are no private agencies operating in this area which conduct recreation programs.

6. Commercial recreation facilities are very limited.

Recommendations

At a meeting of the supervisory staff, the Supervisor of Programs distributed mimeographed copies of his evaluations and findings and reported verbally the views of various persons. The area supervisor was asked to report on his observation visits during the season, on the area meetings, and the center staff discussions. After serious consideration of all factors, the supervisory staff made the following recommendations to the head of the department:

1. Continue the afternoon and Saturday program and add at least one activity.

2. Continue the evening program for another year; then reevaluate and close the center if there is no better receptivity of the program.

3. Through questionnaires and conferences with adults and teenagers, attempt to determine the desires and interests of the new constituency and program accordingly.

4. Improve the publicity program and publicize the availability of facilities for permit group meetings.

5. Request the P.T.A. and leading citizens and existing organizations in the neighborhood to take an active part in promoting the center program, for there is a definite need of service in this area.

How do you know if you have a good or just fair recreation center program? Is attendance the only means of judging a program's success? Surely, if no one participates in a program, you have a first class flop. But what about the half filled room?

Methods for careful evaluation of recreation programs are coming. Through your continuing education program, these evaluation methods will be available to you.

WEEKLY AND MONTHLY REPORTS

Center directors are responsible for the proper preparation and submission of weekly attendance and monthly evaluation reports. The monthly report is due the last day of the month. If it should fall on Saturday, the report is due the Friday before and figures can be turned in on Monday. The monthly narrative evaluation will be an objective report with an honest evaluation.

All the late nights, extra weekends and double checking are not reported. But unless you put down on this monthly report the facts—and tell it like it is—your supervisors will not know what has happened in your center. Your report is seen by supervisors and administrators who have not seen your center in operation. Put your best but honest salesmanship into this report.

Instructions for completing and writing these reports follow. If monthly reporting is incomplete and inadequate, center staff will be required to report semi-monthly. The narrative report is to include:
1. General Activities:
   a. Grade School, Junior High, etc.
   b. Attendance figures

2. Special Interest Activities:
   a. Ladies Night, Slenderella, Puppetry, etc.
   b. Attendance figures
3. Membership and Attendance:
   a. Total attendance
   b. Membership—grade, junior high, senior high, young adults
4. Summary:
   a. Give your opinions
   b. Note your program's effectiveness

DIRECTIONS FOR USING DAILY ATTENDANCE REPORT

1. Under column marked "program," list each separate program offered during the week; e.g., baton lessons, children's crafts, grade school time, Saturday afternoon recreation, junior high night.
2. "Registration"—indicate the total number of individuals registered for the specific program. There will be no entry under "registration" for general recreational activities.
3. "Attendance"—indicate the number, by sex, who were present for that activity. Total of this column for the week should equal total signatures in sign-in book.
4. "Day of week"—indicate M, T, W, Th, F, S, Sun.
5. "A.M.," "P.M.," "eve"—indicate time of day activity was conducted.
6. "Membership," "member bro't fwd"—give last week's total membership for age group.
7. "Membership," "new memb"—indicate number of memberships sold this week for the age group.
8. "Total membership"—add membership brought forward, and New Members.

9. Total all columns except Program, Day of Week, and A.M., P.M., and Eve.

> NOTE: If an activity is offered more than once during the week, please list exact time it is offered. If there is a fee attached to an activity, the registration number should be equal to the number of participants who have paid the fee. (Daily attendance report is shown in Appendix)

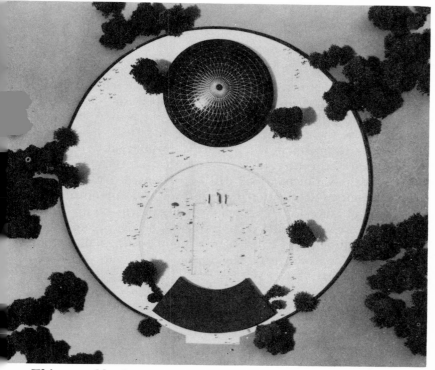

This movable dome can convert the outdoor swimming pool to a covered all-year pool.

ADULT ADVISORY COUNCIL

Each recreation center has an adult advisory council that assists the center director in planning the center program. The following is a list of the bylaws under which the councils operate.

Purpose

The purpose of the Recreation Center Adult Advisory Council will be to assist the center Director in every way possible in the promotion of a popular and worthwhile recreation program.

Membership

Advisory councils shall be organized by each center director with consultation with the Supervisor of Centers and Playgrounds. Membership shall not be less than six nor more than fifteen members. Proposals for new members to the council will be made by mutual agreement between the center director and the Advisory Council. (These recommendations will be presented to the Superintendent of Recreation for approval and appointment.) Term of office for the council members will be for three years except for initial appointments. At the organization of the council, one-third of the membership shall be appointed for three years, one-third for two years, and one-third for one year.

Any member who absents himself from three consecutive meetings shall be considered inactive and asked to resign.

Officers

The Advisory Council shall elect its own chairman, vice-chairman, and secretary who shall serve in this capacity one annual term and who may be reelected *for not more than* one additional consecutive term.

DUTIES
1. Chairman—presides at all meetings of the Recreation Center Adult Advisory Council and performs other duties that are normally associated with chairmanship.
2. Vice-Chairman—acts as chairman in chairman's absence.
3. Secretary—takes the minutes of all proceedings of all meetings. Sends notices to members concerning meetings and writes all necessary correspondence.

Rules and Regulations

Any rules or regulations by the Advisory Council for its own guidance shall in all cases be within the framework of this directive and subject to approval of the Superintendent of Recreation.

Meetings

Meetings shall be held monthly at a time agreed upon by the center director and the advisory council.

Function of Advisory Council

The Advisory Council shall assist the center director in planning recreation programs that will encourage the greatest number of persons of all ages to engage in a variety of suitable activities. These objectives can be implemented by:
1. Interpreting recreation needs to the neighborhood community.

2. Assisting in planning and carrying out special recreation events, holiday celebrations, pageants, open house, demonstrations.
3. Providing opportunity for combined public opinion and professional skill in the solution of neighborhood recreation needs.
4. Considering suggestions and criticisms and making recommendations.

It is expected that the members of the Advisory Council will be persons generally sympathetic to the principles and objectives of community recreation and that they will be guided by a sincere interest in helping to promote a well-rounded, progressive recreation program for the community as a whole.

The value of an Advisory Council to the recreation center can scarcely be exaggerated. Its function, in an advisory capacity, in matters of program is one of the most important services any group of citizens can render the neighborhood community.

Standing Committees

Publicity Committee—the function of this committee will be to assist in the distribution of information concerning the center's facilities and programs.

Volunteer Committee—the function of this committee will be to help secure volunteers to assist in the conducting of the recreation program.

1. Decorating—the function of this committee will be to help assist in the planning for parties and special events held at the center.
2. Refreshment—the function of this committee will be to assist in the planning and securing of refreshments for parties and special activities held at the center.

Special Events Committee—the function of this committee will be to assist in the planning and executing of special events at the center, such as dances, fairs, senior citizens, parties, etc.

Sample Constitution

CONSTITUTION OF AN ADVISORY COUNCIL*

ARTICLE I

The name of this group shall be known as the Recreation Advisory Council of ———— Center.

ARTICLE II

The objectives of the Recreation Advisory Council through their committee shall be:

a. To promote, encourage and advise with respect to cultural, recreational and social activities for the members of the ———— Recreation Center, within the framework of the rules and regulations set forth by the Board of Recreation and Park Commissioners.

b. To enlist the support of the community for the program of the ———— Recreation Center.

c. To serve as a resource in determining community recreation needs.

d. To aid in the recruitment and screening of volunteers in assisting program.

e. To assist the Center Director in the evaluation of Center activities.

f. To observe the program in an advisory capacity.

g. To assist the Center Director with the publicity of the Center.

h. To engage in activities that will further enrich the Center program.

i. To assist in the planning and presentation of special events.

---

* Copy in italics is explanatory.

ARTICLE III

Headquarters

Headquarters will be located at the _____ Recreation Center, _____ (address) _____, and all regular and committee meetings will be held at that location.

Among the reasons why advisory councils fail are:
1. *Factions develop within the group.*

   This can easily occur if it becomes habitual for committee members to meet in one another's homes. Some of the unfortunate effects of this are:
   — *Other committee chairmen feel obligated to hold meetings in their homes too, and are unwilling to do so.*
   — *If a committee chairman does not follow the pattern of meetings in her home, some members feel they are not welcome there, or that there are class or ethnic distinctions.*
   — *Refreshments become more and more elaborate as time progresses and a spirit of competition arises among committee chairmen.*
2. *The tendency develops to call "private" meetings over "emergency" matters. This tends to undermine the function of the council.*
3. *The Center Director gradually loses contact with groups meeting in one another's homes and the council becomes a separate isolated entity.*

ARTICLE IV

Membership

a. The membership of the Recreation Advisory Council shall be composed of any civic minded adult, regardless of racial, religious or ethnic background, willing to devote time and effort for the benefit of the Center. Membership shall be as truly representative of the community as possible. Effort should be made to have representatives from the PTA of nearby schools, and from all local community organizations.

A recreation center can only be successful if it serves the needs and interests of the entire neighborhood or community. Therefore, an Advisory Council must represent all aspects of the community—all races, religions, age groups, and all educational and economic levels.
Councils formed entirely from the power structure of the community (politicians, doctors, lawyers, key businessmen, etc.) often have no real contact with the center and members do not come to meetings.

b. No member of the professional staff shall be a member of the Recreation Advisory Council.

c. Membership in the Recreation Advisory Council includes parents of Center members in the various age groups.

Since one of the functions of a council is to advise on program, it is essential that there not be an imbalance of interest. For example, if all members of the Advisory Council have children in the 7 to 9 year age group, there will be a tendency to neglect the teen-age program. Also, in the fund raising aspects the teen program will perhaps receive less aid.

d. Applications for membership shall be submitted to the Recreation Advisory Council at a regular meeting and referred to the Membership Committee. Applications for membership shall be considered by the Membership Committee and its recommendations submitted to the Recreation Advisory Council at the meeting following the proposal. Membership shall be voted upon by the Recreation

Advisory Council.

e. Any member who fails to attend three consecutive meetings without just cause shall be notified of pending suspension from membership. The Secretary shall inform this member in writing that unless he attends the next regular meeting of the Council his membership shall be terminated. A majority vote of the Council may reinstate to full status any member whose membership has been terminated.

A successful council must consist of active and interested members. If members are permitted to drop out without replacement, the following occurs:
— *The burden of work increases for the remaining members and may cause them to withdraw.*
— *Control of the council is left in the hands of a few.*
— *Voting is not representative of the entire structure of the community.*
— *Exchange of ideas is limited to a few viewpoints.*

f. Regular members shall serve for a period of three years. After an intervening term of one year, they may be eligible for reelection. During this one intervening term, members may continue to participate on the Board of Directors as non-voting and non-office-holding participants.

For a beginning council, some mathematical arrangement will have to be made to carry out the three year term.
This clause is important, however, because:
— *It ensures new blood on the council.*
— *It prevents long-established cliques.*
— *It prevents a situation in which new members are not truly accepted by the "old guard" and are given no leadership responsibility.*

ARTICLE V

Officers

a. The officers shall consist of a President, First Vice President, Second Vice President, Recording Secretary, Corresponding Secretary and Treasurer.

b. Officers shall be elected for a period of one year. An officer may, upon election, succeed himself for the following term. An intervening term must precede a third term in any office. During this intervening term they shall be non-voting, non-office-holding participants.

1. *The need to replace an unsuccessful officer and the resultant formation of defensive "for" and "against" factions will not arise with the short one year term. On the other hand, a valuable officer can succeed himself.*

2. *If there is no change in officers for an extended time:*
   — *There is a tendency for a clique to develop among officers and their appointed chairmen of committees.*
   — *Other members begin to feel that the same people are always "running things."*
   — *No advantage is taken of fresh ideas and new blood.*
   — *Opportunities for leadership are confined to a few.*

ARTICLE VI

Elections

a. There shall be a Nominating Committee consisting of five members; two appointed by the President of the Recreation Advisory Council and three elected by the membership. No member of the Nominating Committee may run for elected office. The Nominating Committee shall present a slate of nominees to the membership at the May meeting of the Recreation Advisory Council. At this meeting, any member of the Recreation Advisory Council may add to the list of nominees. However, no name may be deleted from the slate of officers presented by the Nominating Committee. The Nominating Committee shall elect its own Chairman.

b. Elections shall be held by closed ballot at the June meeting.

c. Installation of officers shall take place at the September meeting.

d. The term of an officer shall be from September 1 through August 31.

Thus, if there is a summer program (the planning for which takes place in the spring), there will be coordination of plans and approach.

Duties of Officers

1. *President*—The President shall preside at all meetings. He shall appoint all Chairmen of Committees (with the exception of the Nominating Committee).

People are often reluctant to volunteer as chairmen of committees, even though they are particularly suited for the task.

Voting on committee chairman positions sometimes runs along social or sentimental lines because there is less strong feeling than with major officers.

Members of committees shall be appointed by the respective committee chairmen.

Chairmen will accomplish more with a committee of friends.

The President shall be an ex-officio member of all committees except the Nominating Committee.

He shall formulate the agenda for meetings in consultation with the Center Director and officers of the Recreation Advisory Council.

2. *First Vice President*—The First Vice President shall assist the President in the performance of his duties and shall act as the President in the President's absence.

3. *Second Vice President*—The Second Vice President shall assist the President in the performance of his duties and shall act as President in the absence of the President and the First Vice President.

Both Vice Presidents shall be ex-officio members of all committees except the Nominating Committee.

4. *Recording Secretary*—The Recording Secretary shall keep an accurate record of the proceedings of all regular and special meetings of the Recreation Advisory Council, and shall perform such other duties connected with the office as the President may direct.

Minutes of meetings are essential to the efficient operation of any organization because:
— *They provide a history and record of the past for new officers.*
— *They provide background information of the center should there be a change in Center Director or Supervisor.*
— *They prevent arguments about what took place at past meetings and what decisions were agreed upon. Such arguments again cause factions and undermine the council.*

5. *Corresponding Secretary*—The Corresponding Secretary shall notify all the members of the Recreation Advisory Council of all regular and special meetings thereforth, and shall attend to all correspondence thereof. A copy of all correspondence dealing with program, organization, policy or center services shall be given to the

Director of the center prior to its being mailed.

The Corresponding Secretary shall perform such other duties connected with his work as directed by the President of the Recreation Advisory Council.

> *It is most important that the Center Director see all correspondence dealing with program, center organization, policy and center services before it is mailed because:*
> — *He can correct errors due to a misunderstanding or misinterpretation of Recreation and Park Commission policies.*
> — *He will be "up-to-date" on the council's activities.*
> — *He will be able to foresee possible problem situations by the content and tone of letters.*
> — *One of the reasons why advisory councils fail is because they antagonize the community by making unfulfilled promises or misrepresenting the facts. The Center Director can catch these mistakes before they are sent out.*
>
> *For example, if an Advisory Council should write in a publicity release that "the center's summer program serves kindergarten children," the Center Director's office will be filled with requests to register four year olds, and he will then be in a position of having to refuse and, at the same time, having to contradict the publicity of his own council. Had he seen the release before it was published, he would have added the age limit qualifications.*

6. *Treasurer*—The Treasurer shall receive all monies and shall keep an accurate, up-to-date record thereof. He shall give an accounting at all meetings and shall put out monies only as authorized by the President. Any expenditure in excess of twenty-five dollars shall require the approval of the Recreation Advisory Council. All checks

for the disbursement of funds shall be signed by both the Treasurer and President.

The Treasurer shall arrange for the books to be audited once a year by an accountant, or by a finance committee, which shall not include the President or Treasurer.

The auditing of books is a protection for those handling the money.

ARTICLE VII

Committees

a. Representation of the Recreation Advisory Council must always be made by no less than two members of any committee, appointed by the Chairman of the respective committee, with the approval of the President.

This clause is most important because:
— It prevents one member from acting in the council's name without its knowledge or sanction.
— It avoids embarrassing the council members by unsanctioned representation. This embarrassment often causes the most valuable members to drop out rather than be associated with the unfavorable impression given other organizations by the unauthorized representative.
— It prevents prejudice. When a leadership team of at least two persons is responsible for a mission and fails, then blame for that failure cannot be laid to race, creed, etc. Prejudice always undermines a council and contributes to the formation of unhealthy factions.

b. There shall be the following standing Committees: Membership Committee, Program and Evaluation Committee, Public Relations Committee, Fund Raising Committee, and Nominating Committee.

c. Additional Committees may be formed according to need.

> *Possible committees:*
> *Recruitment and Screening of Volunteers*
> *Special Events*
> *Clerical Assistance*
> *Community Research*

d. Chairmen of Committees shall be appointed by the President. Chairmen may then appoint the members of their Committee. There shall be at least three members to each committee, including the Chairman.

e. The term of office for a Committee Chairman shall be one year. The Chairman may, upon election, succeed himself for the following term. An intervening term must precede a third term in the same office.

> *Should a committee Chairman be unsuccessful in his task, there will be no need to replace him (thus antagonizing his friends and encouraging the development of undesirable "for and against" factions). He can serve his year, and leave without embarrassment.*
>
> *However, should the Chairman be exceptionally successful, he can serve as committee head for two years, and then be made head of another committee for the intervening term so that his leadership will not be lost.*

Program and Evaluation Committee

It shall be the function of the Program and Evaluation Committee to advise the Center Director on matters concerning the quality and improvement of program for the Recreation Center.

Visits made to the center for the purposes of evaluating the program shall be made only by members of this committee. At least two-thirds of the members of the committee must be present during an evaluation visit. In order to ensure that all age groups of members are adequately represented on the Program and Evaluation Committee, effort should be made to include as members at least one parent of a member in each age group category (kindergarten, elementary school, junior high school and high school) and representatives of the Adult and Senior Citizen groups.

The requirement that two-thirds of the Committee be present during an evaluation visit prevents a "one-sided" report by a few with special interests, and ensures a more complete representation of the needs and interests of the community.

The Program and Evaluation Committee shall make at least three evaluation visits per year. The days of these visits shall be determined by the Committee without consultation with the Center Director and shall be at different times of the year and at different hours of the day in order to be sure that the Committee will observe the Center in its various aspects.

Discussion, criticism and evaluation should be reserved for the meeting of the Recreation Advisory Council or of the Committee.

It is upsetting to the Director, staff and participants if criticism is made during a program session. Nor is it the function of the committee to deal directly with staff.

The Committee members should request an individual conference with the Center Director regarding their evaluation or their suggestions for program.

The method of carrying out the suggestions of the Program and Evaluation Committee shall be the responsibility of the Center Director.

Public Relations Committee

It shall be the function of the Public Relations Committee to maintain a liaison with the neighborhood or community.

This Committee shall also be concerned with publicizing the center's activities.

All publicity inaugurated by the Public Relations Committee shall be reviewed by the Center Director.

> *Review by the Center Director:*
> — *Prevents misinterpretation of Recreation and Park Commission policies.*
> — *Prevents the committee from making promises to the community which it cannot keep.*
> — *Prevents duplication, which antagonizes newspapers, etc., and makes them less willing to publicize center activities in the future.*

Fund Raising Committee

It shall be the function of the Fund Raising Committee to inaugurate and carry out fund raising affairs and to promote donations of materials which can be used in center program.

These fund raising affairs must conform to Recreation and Park Commission regulations.

The disposition of funds raised for the Center shall be determined by a vote of the Recreation Advisory Council.

Membership Committee

All applicants for membership in the Recreation Advisory Council shall be submitted to the Membership Committee for their recommendation. Membership Committee shall submit to the Recreation Advisory Council their recommendation for acceptance or rejection. Reasons for rejection of applicants shall be made known to the Recreation Advisory Council upon request.

ARTICLE VIII

Meetings

a. Meetings shall be conducted according to Roberts Rules of Order Revised.

b. All meetings are to take place at the Recreation Center, _____

(address)

Reasons for this clause are given earlier.

c. There shall be a minimum of six meetings per year.

However, among the reasons why advisory councils fail are:

— *Meetings are called for no apparent reason and members feel that their time has been wasted.*

— *There is no "follow through"—no sense of progress.*

— *There is too great a time between meetings and members lose interest or feel they are not needed.*

— *Plans are too vast and are unsuccessful because they cannot be properly carried out.*

— *The Center Director "takes over" the meeting.*

— *There is a lack of basic human needs for members of the Council:*
success
satisfaction
security
status
sense of belonging
recognition
new experiences

— *Meetings are held in poor facilities (too cold, too many stairs to climb, too dark, etc.).*

— *There are no social aspects (no refreshments, no time for individual exchange of greetings and news).*

— *Not every member is given a part to play.*

d. A special meeting of the Recreation Advisory Council may be called by the President at any time provided that five days' prior notice in writing be transmitted to all members of the Council.

e. Discussion and decision must move according to the wishes of the majority.

This prevents the meeting from being interrupted by someone who has "an axe to grind," or who has a pet project in which no one else is interested.

f. Items for discussion may be presented by either the Recreation Advisory Council or by the Center Director.

g. All decisions shall be made on the basis of compiled information that has been considered by the appropriate committee.

This clause prevents prejudiced viewpoints from leading the Council to false conclusions.

h. The Center Director shall be present at each meeting of the Recreation Advisory Council as a resource person and a non-voting member. He shall never serve in the capacity of an Officer or Chairman and shall not become a member of any committee.

i. A quorum shall consist of —— members, including the President or Vice Presidents.

ARTICLE IX

Amendments

This Constitution may be amended at any regular meeting of the Recreation Advisory Council, provided that a copy of the proposed amendment has been submitted to each member in writing, and said amendment has been read to the Recreation Advisory Council at any regular meeting prior to the voting thereof.

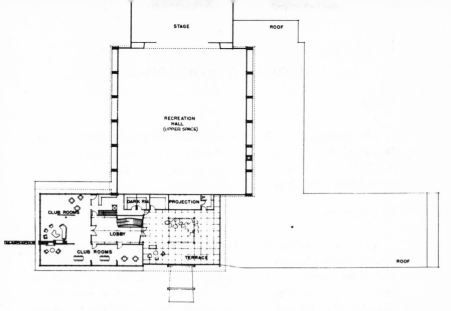

Bowling alleys, game rooms, stages and the second floor lobby of this recreation center present unique operational problems.

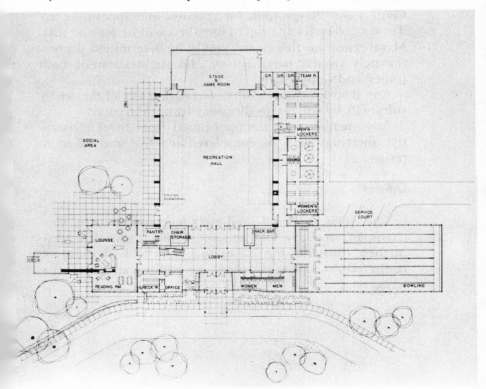

JUNIOR ADVISORY BOARD

Purpose

The purpose of the Recreation Center Junior Advisory Board will be to assist the Center Director in every way possible in the promotion of a popular and worthwhile recreation program.

Membership

Advisory Boards shall be organized by each Center Director with consultation with the Supervisor of Centers and Playgrounds. Membership shall not be less than six nor more than fifteen members. Proposals for new members to the Board will be made by mutual agreement between the Center Director and the Board. (These recommendations will be presented to the Supervisor of Centers and Playgrounds for approval and appointment.) Term of office for the Board members will be for one year. Membership on this Board should be determined proportionately to the participation and registration of both junior and senior high.

Any Board member guilty of violating any of the center rules will be subject to dismissal from the center.

Any member who absents himself from three consecutive meetings shall be considered inactive and asked to resign.

Officers

The Advisory Board shall elect its own chairman, vice-chairman, secretary, and assistant secretary who shall serve in these capacities for one annual term and who may be re-elected *for not more than* one additional consecutive term.

DUTIES:

1. Chairman—presides at all meetings of the Board and performs other duties that are normally associated with Chairmanship.
2. Vice-Chairman—presides in absence of the Chairman.
3. Secretary—takes the minutes of all proceedings of all meetings. Sends notices to members concerning meetings and writes all necessary correspondence.
4. Assistant Secretary—takes minutes in the absence of the Secretary.

Rules and Regulations

Any rules or regulations by the Junior Advisory Board for its own guidance shall in all cases be within the framework of this directive and subject to the approval of the Superintendent of Recreation.

Meetings

Meetings shall be held monthly or bi-monthly at a time agreed upon by the Center Director and the Center Advisory Board.

Function of Advisory Board

The Advisory Board shall assist the Center Director in planning recreation programs that will encourage the greatest number of persons of all ages to engage in a variety of suitable activities. These objectives can be implemented by:

1. Interpreting recreation needs to the neighborhood community.
2. Assisting in planning and carrying out special recreation events, holiday celebrations, pageants, open

house, demonstrations.

3. Providing opportunity for combined public opinion and professional skill in the solution of neighborhood recreation needs.
4. Consider suggestions and criticisms and make recommendations.

It is expected that the members of the Junior Advisory Board will be persons generally sympathetic to the principles and objectives of community recreation and that they will be guided by a sincere interest in helping to promote a well-rounded, progressive recreation program for the community as a whole.

The value of a Junior Advisory Board to the recreation center can scarcely be exaggerated. Its function, in an advisory capacity, in matters of program is one of the most important services any group of citizens can render the neighborhood community.

Standing Committees

Decorating Committee—the function of this committee will be to assist in the planning for parties and special events held at the recreation center.

Publicity Committee—the function of this committee will be to assist in the distribution of information concerning the center facilities and programs.

Refreshment Committee—the function of this committee will be to assist in the planning and securing of refreshments for parties and special activities held at the center.

Volunteer Committee—the function of this committee will be to help secure volunteers to assist in the conducting of the recreation programs.

Special Events Committee—the function of this committee will be to assist in the planning and executing of special events at the center, such as dances, fairs, senior citizens, parties, etc.

NOTE: The above committees may be combined if deemed necessary by the Junior Advisory Board members.

REQUISITION FOR SUPPLIES

Purchase of items costing over $15.00 must be requested through the Supervisor of Centers on a "Request for Purchase" form as shown in the Appendix. This is to be used for items not concerned with maintenance (band requests, program equipment, etc.). All purchases under $15.00 will be made through the use of purchase order books obtained from the office bookkeeper.

AWARDS

Awards may be given for contests and events. These may consist of material items such as trophies, games, and equipment, or free tickets to special events. Money may not be used as an award. All awards are to be approved by the Recreation Commission.

HOURS OF OPERATION

The following are the hours for the operation of the recreation centers:
1. 9:00 A.M. until 10:30 P.M., Monday through Friday; 9:00 A.M. until 11:00 P.M. Saturday.
2. Schedule within framework of No. 1. Exceptions must be approved by the Supervisor of Centers.

PROCEDURES FOR CLOSING FACILITIES

Center personnel will develop a check list for the procedures of closing the facility prior to the closing for the day. This check list will include checking all doors and windows and locking them, checking all rooms and areas to assure that all participants have departed, turning out all lights, and unplugging all electrical appliances that are not required to operate during the period the center is closed. It is the responsibility of the center director to be sure proper instruction has been given to staff members in charge of closing the facility.

FACILITY RESERVATIONS

The recreation center will not be reserved for other than normal programming without the specific authorization of the Superintendent of Recreation or his designated representative. Individuals requesting facility reservations will be asked to submit a written application to the Superintendent of Recreation (form shown in Appendix) listing facilities desired, time, use, number of participants, etc. The Superintendent will answer such requests in writing.

The recreation center will be made available on the following priority list:

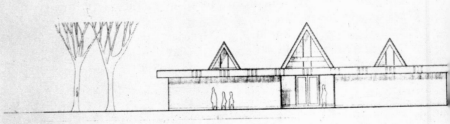

SOUTH ELEVATION

This is an artist's concept of the proper size and height of a building in relationship to man.

1. Programs and activities sponsored and conducted by the Recreation Commission under leadership of its staff.
2. Groups, clubs, or associations working or affiliated with the Recreation Commission. For example, senior citizen clubs, bridge club, etc.
3. School sponsored activity groups and clubs.
4. Other community non-profit recreation groups having open membership such as the Square Dance Association, the Antique Car Club, the Coin Club, etc.

The building will be made available free of charge; however, when it is necessary to employ personnel to supervise when it is in use by one of these clubs, a charge will be made for this cost. If janitorial services are required to clean the facility following its use, a charge for this person will also be made; however, if a group desires to assume this responsibility, no charge will be made.

A record of usage by outside groups must be kept at times when additional personnel are required as it is necessary to send the user a statement of cost.

DUTIES OF POLICEMEN

1. Report to Center Director at designated time.
2. Remain outside at a location that allows you to observe the maximum amount of building and area and in a position where patrons arriving at the building will see you.
3. Make at least three trips around the building each hour.
4. Do not allow loitering about the outside of the building; groups that form should be dispersed.
5. Report unusual incidents or individuals to the Center Director.

6. Do not smoke while on station; the Director will make arrangements for break periods.
7. Do not allow persons to smoke within 50 feet of the building.
8. The parking lot should be checked at least twice each hour.
9. Perform other duties as outlined by the Center Director; he will give you a written list of trouble spots and other areas of concern.

BULK MAILOUTS

Bulk mailout envelopes are not to be used for any mailouts numbering *less than 200 pieces*. They are not to be used for first-class materials; they may be used when sending bulletins, form letters, etc. The bulk mailings must *first* go through the Recreation Commission office before being sent to the Post Office.

4

PERSONNEL

Your job description should show accurately what you are expected to do. If you do not have a written job description you should begin to assemble it now. PROPER ASSIGNMENT OF DUTIES THROUGH A JOB DESCRIPTION HELPS TO AVOID PROBLEMS WITH SUPERVISORS AND FELLOW WORKERS.

JOB DESCRIPTIONS FOR CENTER PERSONNEL

Center Director

The Recreation Center Director is responsible for the conduct of a comprehensive recreation program for a single recreation center which usually includes a recreation building, playground, swimming pool, and tennis courts.

DUTIES AND RESPONSIBILITIES OF THE RECREATION CENTER DIRECTOR:

1. Has full charge of the operation of the program, staff, and facilities.
2. Plans and administers a diversified recreation pro-

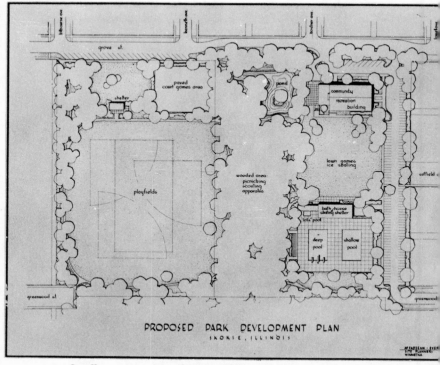

PROPOSED PARK DEVELOPMENT PLAN
SKOKIE, ILLINOIS

Staffing of recreation facilities increases when the physical structures are separate.

gram suited to the needs of the participants and potential participants within the framework of policies set forth by the Recreation Commission; schedules and directs the use of the facility without close or continuous supervision.

3. Assigns duties to, supervises, and evaluates all personnel at the recreation center including professional, part-time, seasonal, and volunteer.

4. Oversees maintenance of the facility; inspects fa-

cility, equipment, and program activities for safety; directs the correction of unsafe physical or program conditions.

5. Requisitions and justifies purchase or building of equipment for center use.

6. Maintains and submits to the supervisor accurate financial, personnel, and program service records; participates in the budget-making process, makes recommendations for center budget, and submits it with supporting data.

7. Studies, analyzes, and evaluates program, participation and attendance, leadership, and personnel, and recommends and reports needed action.

8. Promotes, organizes, and stimulates good relationships with neighborhood and activity interest groups and with other agencies serving the area; interprets the center program and its philosophy to groups and individuals through personal activity.

9. Publicizes center activities, events, and programs through appropriate media and with the approval of the supervisor.

10. Organizes and leads groups in recreation activities, recruits and trains volunteer leadership.

11. Carries out other duties as assigned.

Assistant Recreation Center Director

Under the supervision of the Recreation Center Director, the Assistant Center Director is responsible for personal direction of assigned portions of the recreation program, aids in the administration of the center, supervises part-time recreation leaders and seasonal personnel whether paid or volunteer, and acts for the Center Director in his absence.

DUTIES AND RESPONSIBILITIES:

1. Assists the Center Director in the administration of

a diversified recreation center program, directs assigned segments of the program, and leads activities suited to the needs and interests of those attending the center.

2. Assists the Director in supervision of maintenance; inspects the facility, equipment, and program activities for safety; reports and oversees the correction of unsafe physical or program conditions as assigned.

3. Maintains, reviews, and analyzes records of center finance, equipment, program, and personnel for the Director as assigned; requisitions and justifies purchase or building of equipment for center use.

4. Promotes and participates in maintaining good relationships with neighborhood activity interest groups and with the other agencies serving the area, as directed, but with some latitude for initiative and judgment in application of policy.

5. Organizes and leads groups in recreation activities, recruits and trains volunteer leadership as directed.

6. Carries out other duties as assigned.

RULES OF CONDUCT FOR PERSONNEL

Dress

Jeans—blue or otherwise—are not considered appropriate wear for center personnel.

Male personnel—dress pants, shirt, and tie are considered minimum standards while working in the center. Suit or sport coat is appropriate and creates a favorable impression.

Female personnel—slacks and shorts are not to be worn by female center personnel except when actually engaged in conducting classes that demand such wear. Skirt, blouse, and hose are considered as minimum standards.

This recreation center is compact with two floors providing the craft and meeting rooms.

Participation in Activities

Because the center staff are considered leaders—not participants—in all programs conducted at the center, personnel on duty will not participate in activities other than to initiate or create interest in an activity. Instruction in activities should be presented in advance.

Promptness for Work

Recreation centers must be opened and closed as scheduled. Any variation must be approved in advance by the Supervisor of Centers and Playgrounds.

Smoking

Students are not permitted to smoke in the building. Staff, adults, and volunteer smoking will be confined to designated area.

Unexcused Absences

Notification must be made to the office if you must be out of town during the time when the center is in operation.

Compensatory Time

No additional pay is given for overtime. Approval of the compensatory time will be made at the time of the request for additional work.

Personal Liability

Staff may be held personally liable for negligent acts while conducting activities.

Workmen's Compensation

(The compensation program below reflects only one state's requirements. Make sure you check your State Workmen's Compensation. Each state has different requirements for coverage.)

In the event of an accident or occupational disease,

follow these steps:

1. *Notify your employer immediately.* This necessitates the completion of an Employee's Accident Report Form to be turned in *immediately.*

2. Follow the doctor's instructions at all times. Your employer is obligated to furnish necessary medical and hospital expenses to the amount of $6000. If the services of the physician or surgeon furnished by the employer are not satisfactory to the injured workman, the workman may without approval of the Director consult another physician or surgeon of his choice and the employer shall pay the fees to the extent of $100.

3. You are not entitled to compensation for the first week's disability. Thereafter you are entitled to 60 percent of your average weekly wages for the period of total disability—not less than $7 nor more than $42 per week. If the injury results in permanent disability, the state compensation law provides for additional benefits.

4. Written claim for compensation must be made upon your employer within 180 days of the date of accident or date of last employment of compensation. If your disability resulted from an occupational disease, you have 90 days in which to serve notice and one year from the date your disability began in which to serve written claim. If claim is not made, your rights to compensation may be prejudiced.

5. Your employer has been supplied with cards showing maximum benefits provided by the compensation law. He will explain these benefits upon request.

STAFF MEETINGS

Staff meetings are held on the second and fourth Mon-

Observation decks within recreation centers are provided for the comfort of spectators.

days from 1:00 through 3:00 P.M. All full-time and part-time personnel working 25 or more hours per week are required to attend. The purpose is to discuss current problems of personnel and to obtain other information necessary for operation of the program. Staff are responsible for bringing summary of past activities and special events and future plans to the meeting and are to be prepared to discuss items on the agenda.

IN-SERVICE TRAINING

Orientation—General

1. Observe recreational facilities

2. Observe center programs in action
3. Meet other center personnel and office staff

Work Under Supervision

1. Rotation from center to center helping personnel do program
2. Reports
3. Lock-up

Recommendations

1. Conferences—every possible means should be obtained to go to conferences such as the Midwest District Conference
2. Professional literature
3. Professional speakers
4. Recreation sources at colleges and universities

HOURS OF WORK

An effort will be made to give all full-time employees a 40 hour work week.

PART-TIME PERSONNEL

1. All part-time employees must complete an application of employment—forms may be obtained at the recreation office.
2. All part-time employees must be at least 16 years of age.
3. Part-time employees should be paid a minimum federal, state or local minimum wage and a maximum not to exceed the hourly equivalent of a full time person performing the same job.

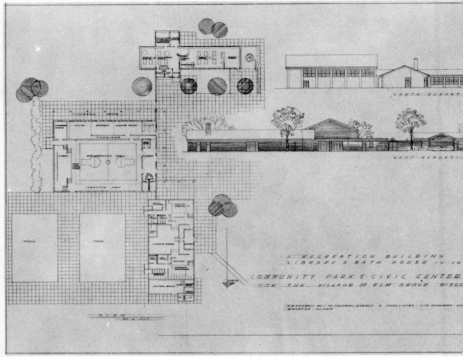

Branch or small libraries are often included in recreation centers. The library usually occupies the upper floor or an attached wing.

4. All part-time employees will be required to complete a weekly time card and submit it to the center director. The time card is to include the following information:
   a. Name, as listed on social security card
   b. Title
   c. Payroll period (1–15; 16–30/31 for full-time) (11–25; 26–10 for part-time)
   d. Total hours worked per day (breakdown of hours worked, i.e. 9–12, 1–3, 7–11)

e. Total hours per pay period. (Persons on hourly wage should indicate rate of pay per hour.)

5. When it is necessary for a center to employ part-time leadership, only persons approved by the Supervisor of Centers and Playgrounds may be employed.

VOLUNTEERS

Volunteer leaders play an important part in community centers. They add fresh viewpoints, supplement paid staff, and become ambassadors in the community. Below are some helpful hints regarding volunteers.

1. Types—advisory, leadership, non-leadership, clerical or maintenance, miscellaneous (such as chaperons), entertainment.
2. Value—enthusiasm, different viewpoint, perform special functions.
3. Source—experts in recreational activities, participants in various recreational activities, parents, local organizations, personal contact.
4. Training—workshops, center classes.

EVALUATION OF EMPLOYEES

At the end of each six months, all center employees—full-time, part-time, volunteers—will be evaluated. Following is suggested criteria to be used in evaluating. Employees should be rated in each division as *good, fair,* or *poor.*

1. What is the quality of their leadership?
2. Do they use imagination and initiative?
3. Is their personality pleasing for recreation?
4. Do they use good subject matter for particular areas?
5. Do they use good judgment and common sense?

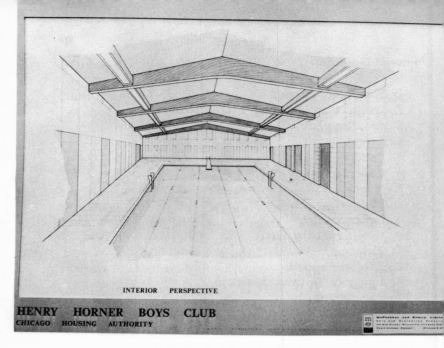

INTERIOR PERSPECTIVE

HENRY HORNER BOYS CLUB
CHICAGO HOUSING AUTHORITY

An indoor swimming pool can easily be added to an existing recreation center.

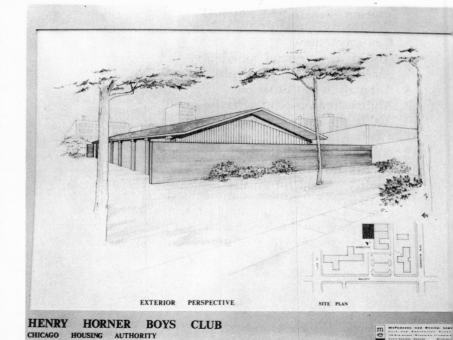

EXTERIOR PERSPECTIVE   SITE PLAN

HENRY HORNER BOYS CLUB
CHICAGO HOUSING AUTHORITY

Personal Qualities

1. Poise and bearing
2. Cooperative attitude
3. Self-discipline
4. Tolerance
5. Patience
6. Concern for others
7. Appearance (dress, neatness, cleanliness)
8. Physical fitness
9. Dependability
10. Willingness to learn
11. Pleasing voice
12. Effective speech
13. Integrity (loyalty, honesty)
14. Promptness

Leadership Qualities

1. Realizes objectives of program
2. Understands and knows needs
3. Gets along well with participants
4. Originality (creative ability)
5. Resourcefulness
6. Ability to command confidence
7. Ability to analyze problems
8. Adaptability to situations
9. Ability to arouse interests
10. Ability to develop interests
11. Leads without dominating
12. Ability to handle disciplinary problems
13. Ability to inspire others
14. Ability to lead informally
15. Initiative

Administrative Qualities

1. Ability to plan
2. Ability to organize
3. Ability to express plans in writing
4. Ability to schedule
5. Ability to supervise others
6. Ability to adapt program
7. Observe rules and regulations
8. Care of equipment and property
9. Constructive contribution at staff meetings
10. Alertness to health needs
11. Orderly clean-up
12. Gets along well with people
13. Ability to use time advantageously
14. Ability to use existing facilities

SPECIAL INSTRUCTIONS TO PERSONNEL

Movie Area

The following instructions supplement the General Instructions to Community Center Personnel. Every instructor should thoroughly familiarize himself with both the General and Special Instructions.

Purpose of Movies. The purpose of the movie program is to provide wholesome entertainment for the Center participants.

Personal Appearance. Boys and girls of the age that participate in the movie program are easily influenced by the leader; therefore, it is essential that the leader's actions and dress set an example. (Sport shirt and slack pants or skirt and blouse are acceptable.)

Care of Room. The audience should not enter the movie

area until it is ready for the seating of the participants. Heating and ventilation should be checked before and during the program to insure the comfort of the participants. Lights should be turned up whenever the audience moves in or out of the area. Care must be taken that aisles are open and without obstruction; neither should anyone or anything be permitted to block the exit doors.

Care of Equipment. The movie leader will be in charge of specific equipment as assigned by the Director. However, all personnel should feel a protective responsibility for the projector, loudspeaker, seats, and other center property. Movie leaders should be thoroughly familiar with the operation of the projector. DO NOT REWIND FILMS.

Audience Control. A reasonable amount of noisy reaction to the pictures is to be expected from the audience as a whole, but rowdyism must be discouraged.

Children must not be permitted to bring food or drinks into movie area.

The Director should instruct all personnel as to their specific duties in case of a fire or an emergency, so as to assure safe conduct of all children to a place of safety. The recreation leader in charge should move about the auditorium at periodic intervals.

GENERAL: THE MOVIE LEADER

1. Under no circumstances should a leader leave his assigned area *unless relieved by the Center Director.*
2. Do not rewind films.
3. *Return film to Center Director only immediately following the show.*
4. If a permanent seating arrangement is not available, the movie leader is responsible for supervising the setting up and taking down of chairs with the aid of the student planning council.
5. The movie leader should report to the Center Director immediately following the show for his assignment for the remainder of the evening.

Active Games Area

The following instructions supplement the General Instructions to Community Center Personnel. Every leader should thoroughly familiarize himself with both the General and Special Instructions.

Purpose of the Activity. The Active Game Room is designed to provide an opportunity for instruction and participation in bowling, pool, nok hockey, kikit and a great variety of active games. Many of these activities are of the type readily transferable to the home because they may be adapted to areas of restricted space.

Care of Equipment. The active games instructor is responsible for setting up and putting away all active games equipment. The storage of active games equipment should be kept in neat order at all times. Incomplete or damaged games should be reported immediately. Requisition game replacements as needed. Keep inventory up to date. The active games instructor should make minor repairs on games when possible which will save many games from total destruction. Emphasis should be placed on the proper care and use of games and equipment.

Care of Rooms or Hallway. Writing and marking on tables, furniture, walls, blackboards, and bulletin board must be prohibited. Day school blackboard work, displays and projects should not be molested.

Personal Appearance. Boys and girls of the age that participate in the active games room activities are easily influenced by the leader; therefore it is essential that the leader's actions and dress set an example (sport shirt and slack pants acceptable; skirt and blouse also acceptable)

GENERAL: THE ACTIVE GAMES ROOM LEADER

1. Shall under no circumstance leave his assigned area *unless relieved by the Center Director.*
2. Shall plan to teach at least one new game each week
3. Shall participate in games only for the purpose of instruction or motivation.

4. Shall develop a working knowledge of the various games in the inventory.
5. Shall move about the room freely in order to encourage participation and check equipment.
6. Shall control boisterousness and over-enthusiastic participants, and teach all participants to share in the responsibility of keeping the room and equipment neat and orderly.
7. Shall have a thorough knowledge of the entire community center program and encourage participants to participate in other activities.
8. Shall experiment with techniques to develop and sustain interest in games through tournaments, bulletin boards, announcements, etc.

Matches and Tournaments. It is advisable to conduct tournaments in bowling, nok hockey, etc. within the Center to create additional interest and enthusiasm in the games.

Intra Center matches in the above activities may be promoted, provided such competition is limited to one match per week.

When conducting tournaments, issue game equipment in such a manner as to reserve some for participants who do not desire to participate in tournament play.

Names, records, and standings of tournament participants should be kept up to date and posted on the active games room bulletin board.

Inventory. At the close of the season, place a slip in each box or attach a slip to each game stating whether the game is complete or incomplete.

Games which have proven obsolete or unpopular should be so labeled.

Gymnasium Area

The following instructions supplement the General Instructions to Community Center Personnel. Every leader should thoroughly familiarize himself with both the General and Special Instructions.

Purpose of the Activity. It is the purpose of the gymnasium program to provide an opportunity for play and instruction in volleyball, basketball, etc. emphasizing good sportsmanship and fair play.

Care of Equipment. Any equipment damaged or in need of repair should be reported to the Center Director.

Care of the Room. Make the gymnasium as safe as possible by seeing that there are no obstructions on the playing court. See that portable seats are properly arranged so as not to interfere with the play.

Report immediately to the Director of the Center any needed repairs to the floor, baskets, blackboards, window guards, window shades, nets, exit lights, etc.

Unless it is necessary to seat spectators on the stage, do not permit anyone on it. The stage scenery, curtains, etc. should be carefully guarded.

Personal Appearance. Gym leaders *should wear tennis shoes,* slack pants, sport shirt or sweat shirt.

General. The Gymnasium Leader

1. Shall under no circumstance, leave his assigned area *unless relieved by the Center Director.*
2. Shall maintain order and proper conduct in the gym at all times.
3. Shall supervise the organization of choose-up play and provide for adequate officiating.
4. Shall not permit participants to congregate in the doorways or halls leading to the gym.
5. Shall not permit any type of gambling.
6. Shall not *permit anyone to play in street shoes.* Tennis shoes are recommended, but play in stocking feet is acceptable.
7. *Shall not hold valuables or other personal property belonging to any participant.*
8. Shall organize and conduct community center leagues and assign competent officials other than himself to

ELMHURST   PARK   DISTRICT   McFADZEAN AND EVERLY LT
ELMHURST ILLINOIS   874 GREENBAY ROA
WINNETKA . ILLINOI

A central entrance and exit allows supervision to be kept to a minimum.

handle games.

9. Shall not grant practice periods to school teams under the name of the school or under any assumed name.

Leagues and Tournaments. Special instructions will be forwarded to the gym instructor regarding the organization and conduct of community center basketball leagues, inter-center match games and tournaments.

Arts and Crafts Area

The following instructions supplement the General Instructions to Community Center Personnel. Every leader should thoroughly familiarize himself with both the General and Special Instructions.

Purpose of the Activity. The purpose of the arts and

crafts program is to provide an opportunity for pleasurable and constructive use of leisure time in a friendly atmosphere; to provide an opportunity to participate in an activity which has a definite carry-over value for hobby interest; to offer an opportunity for self-discovery, self-expression and creativeness at the individual's level of achievement; to provide an opportunity for children to work with a wide variety of arts and crafts materials; and to develop an interest in and a positive attitude toward art and its relation to everyday life.

Fee. The only fee charged in the arts and crafts program is for materials. A cost sheet will be supplied by the arts and crafts supervisor.

Care of Equipment. Arts and Crafts leaders are responsible for the care and neatness of the arts and crafts materials and storage area at the end of the session.

1. Crayons and chalk should be returned to boxes and covered.
2. Paint and paste jar covers should be secured tightly.
3. Water color boxes should be cleaned.
4. Brushes should be thoroughly cleaned before being stored in the storage area.
5. Paper should be neatly stacked.
6. Scissors should be collected and stored in the storage area.

Arts and Crafts leaders are responsible for maintaining an adequate inventory of supplies. Basic and Supplementary Arts and Crafts supplies may be ordered from the Center Director. The arts and crafts leader should order ahead of time, as deliveries are made only once a week. Be careful not to over order.

Make a written list of the supplies desired on a craft order blank (See Request For Purchase Form in Appendix).

Care of the Room. There should be an adequate number of tables and chairs arranged in such a manner as to provide ample working space, the best possible lighting, and accessibility to the leader.

Day school rooms are used for classes. These rooms must be left neat and clean. The last 15 minutes of the session should be set aside for cleaning up, and the children should be trained to leave the room neat and orderly.

Tables should be covered with newsprint or old paper when working with clay, paper mache, paints, or other materials which would mar table tops.

Sinks in which paint brushes are cleaned, etc. should be carefully rinsed before leaving at the end of the session.

Conduct of the Activity. Plan work ahead of time and have materials ready for distribution when the children arrive.

Whenever possible have a sample available of the project to be attempted.

Demonstrate so that all can see.

Exhibit completed work of all children.

Plan an open house or demonstration class for parents to acquaint them with the work done by their children.

Keep an attitude of friendly helpfulness toward all regardless of ability.

Make the art experience a happy, worthwhile experience for all.

Dress. Boys and girls of the age that participate in the arts and crafts program are easily influenced by the leader; therefore, it is essential that the leader's actions and dress set an example. (Sport shirt and slack pants and skirt and blouse are acceptable.)

GENERAL. THE ARTS AND CRAFTS ROOM LEADER

1. Shall, under no circumstance, leave his assigned area *unless relieved by the Center Director.*
2. Shall plan to teach at least one new project each week.

3. Shall move about the room freely in order to encourage participation and check supplies.
4. Shall have a thorough knowledge of the entire community center program and encourage participants to join in other activities.

Dance Area

Record Dance Leader. The following instructions supplement the General Instructions to Community Center Personnel. Every leader should thoroughly familiarize himself with both the General and Special Instructions.

Purpose of the Activity. It is the purpose of the dance program to provide an opportunity for participants to receive instructions in dancing, and an opportunity to socialize.

Care of Equipment. The dance leader will be in charge of records and record players. Dance leaders should be thoroughly familiar with the operation of the record player. Extreme care should be exercised when using this equipment, for it may be damaged very easily.

Personal Appearance. Boys and girls of the age that participate in the dance program are easily influenced by the leader; therefore, it is essential that leader's dress set an example (sport shirt and slacks or skirt and blouse acceptable).

GENERAL. THE DANCE LEADER

1. Shall under no circumstances leave his assigned area *unless relieved by the Center Director.*
2. Shall set up and put away equipment.
3. Shall prevent any conduct that is not proper such as scuffling, running and unruly activity.
4. Shall encourage only acceptable forms of dress.
5. Shall circulate among the dancers and get to know them as individuals as well as letting them get to know him.

Swimming Pool Area

The following instructions supplement the General Instructions to Community Center Personnel. Every leader should thoroughly familiarize himself with both the General and Special Instructions.

Purpose of the Activity. It is the purpose of this activity to provide recreation through swimming and water games.

Personal Appearance. All pool leaders should wear swimming suits so that they will be ready for any emergency.

GENERAL. THE SWIMMING POOL LEADER

1. Shall under no circumstances leave his assigned area *unless relieved by the Center Director.*
2. Shall open and close pool.
3. Shall supervise the locker room.
4. Shall check student numbers between periods.
5. Shall maintain proper order and discipline in the water and on the deck.
6. Shall act as life guard.
7. Shall enforce health rules.

5

FINANCE

ACCOUNTING FOR FUNDS PROCEDURES

Purpose

To establish controls and procedures to account for and safeguard funds collected by the recreation center and craft center.

PROPOSED BUDGET

Salaries and Wages
Director	$8,000.00	
Assistant Director	7,000.00	
Part-Time Personnel	3,000.00	
Custodian—Maintenance	5,000.00	
TOTAL		$23,000.00

Services
Telephone	$ 300.00	
Heat	1,250.00	
Lights	600.00	
Staff Training	200.00	
Program Services	1,000.00	
Printing	200.00	
Hospitalization	650.00	
TOTAL		$ 4,200.00

Supplies and Material
  Office Supplies $ 350.00
  Custodial   250.00
  Concession   800.00
  Program Supplies   400.00
  Miscellaneous   300.00
                   TOTAL $ 2,100.00

Repairs and Maintenance
  Building—Plumbing
  Programs Equipment
  Electrical $1,000.00
                   TOTAL $ 1,000.00

GRAND TOTAL OPERATION $30,300.00

Membership
  50¢ Grades 2–5 $ 500.00
  $1.00 Grades 6–12   2,000.00
  Concessions   1,200.00
  Arts and Crafts Supplies   2,000.00
  Rent of Facilities   1,400.00
  Teenage Dances   ·1,800.00
  Instruction Programs—Adults
                 Children   2,500.00
                   TOTAL $11,400.00

TOTAL COST OF CENTER OPERATION   30,300.00
ANTICIPATED REVENUE   11,400.00
          NET COST OF OPERATION $18,900.00

General

This policy will apply to all funds collected at the center including dues, vending machine revenue, service charges, and others as collected.

Candy and Juke Box Revenue

Funds collected from the candy vending machine and juke box machine will be counted jointly by a representative of the vending machine company and the Center Director or the assistant director. The vendor and Center Director should sign the vendor's receipt and one copy should accompany the Financial Report. All keys to the candy machine and juke box should be turned over to the vending companies.

Soft Drink Machine

The coin collection box of each soft drink machine should be emptied and counted by center personnel at the close of each day's business. An accounting of drinks sold, drinks on hand, and funds collected should be submitted to the center supervisor at the end of each week. (Form is shown in Appendix.)

Disposition of Funds

All funds collected should be placed in a locked bank deposit bag along with a deposit slip. This locked bag should be deposited in the night deposit box at the bank by the Center Director.

Financial Report

Each Center Director is responsible for the financial report and should instruct subordinates in the proper methods of preparation of reports and accounting of funds. The financial report (shown in Appendix) should be submitted to the Recreation Commission along with copies of the deposit slips. Procedures for completing the Financial Report follow:

1. Staple vendor's receipts to top left side of report.
2. Staple all bills on top right side of report, arranged according to size of paper with smallest on top.
3. List bills, starting with top bill (smallest) and continue in order. (If additional space is needed, con-

tinue on back including all required information.)
4. Original deposit slip goes in bag with money. The copy of the deposit slip is to be attached to report.
5. Report is due no later than 2:00 P.M. each Monday to the Supervisor of Centers and Playgrounds.

MEMBERSHIP RECEIPTS

All receipts from the purchase or replacement of membership cards and guest fees shall be entered on the weekly center financial report. At the start of each weekly financial period, the beginning numbers of the five membership card series are recorded. This same procedure is repeated at the end of the period with the ending card numbers. The number of cards sold is the difference between the beginning and ending numbers. To arrive at the sales receipts, the number of cards sold is multiplied by the sales price.

FEES FROM ACTIVITIES

Fees for center activities are paid by two methods. They may be mailed to the Recreation Commission office or submitted directly to the center staff. With either of these methods, an accounting must be made on the weekly center financial record.

CASH REFUNDS OR PAYMENTS

Cash refunds or payments will not be allowed for any reason. When a situation arises that demands that payment be made upon delivery, arrangements should be made to secure a check before the needed date.

This is a recreation center built next to a small lagoon. The multi-purpose room is located on the second floor overlooking the lagoon.

SALES TAX COLLECTION

Sales tax is not to be computed or collected on charges for instructions, lessons, or educational lectures. Examples of these are bridge and craft instructions and baton lessons.

Sales tax should be paid on any sales to individuals of any materials (clay, oils, canvas, etc.) or admission ticket sales (ticket discount books, etc.). Examples: craft supplies, membership tickets to centers, all admissions to all center dances where a fee is charged.

Receipts from the sale of admissions to athletic events, lectures, dances, plays, concerts, and other forms of entertainment sponsored by schools, colleges, or universities, or recreation departments are taxable. This applies whether the admission is sold in the form of a single ticket of admission, a season ticket to a series of lectures, concerts, etc., or as a so called activity ticket which admits to the diversified group of entertainments. An example of this would be the membership cards or fees to the center dances.

Roller skating would not be included because it is below the minimum amount taxable. *Sales tax is only collected on 10 cents or over.* If you have further questions concerning this, inquire at the Recreation office. Each state has different minimum sales and sales tax rates.

FINANCIAL PLANNING WORK SHEET

WHAT: FINANCIAL PLAN AND PREPARATIONS
FOR: YOUNG ADULT PROGRAM (17 thru 20)
WHERE: COMMUNITY CENTER—BASEMENT

	Action Started	Action Completed
1. Building Requirements	———	———
A. Facilities		
(1) Cleaning		
(a) Rooms	———	———
(b) Kitchen	———	———
(c) Bar	———	———
(d) Stairways	———	———
(2) Lighting		
(a) Fluorescent lighting (bar) to be softened	———	———
(b) Fluorescent lighting check room decreased	———	———
(c) Ceiling tubes—with color bulbs—in dancing area—complete other fixtures with bulbs	———	———
(d) Band—stage—still incomplete without black lighting—rheostat switches have not been corrected as requested. I.e.: control for 2 blue—2 red—and center yellow	———	———

	Action Started	Action Completed

(e) P.A. System
    1. To be serviced and conditioned   ———   ———
    2. Speaker (s) to be installed   ———   ———
    3. Record player (45–35–16 RPM) to be attached   ———   ———
    4. Mikes—replaced—or added to set   ———   ———

(f) Barrier (for privacy) to block off men's toilet entrance   ———   ———

(g) Checkroom
    1. Remove wall (attached) section for adequate recess to other racks   ———   ———
    2. Set up secondary racks in storeroom—under sidewalk—for larger attendance   ———   ———
    3. Mark hanger slots—and hangers with numbered markings   ———   ———
    4. Set up number board for hat checking racks   ———   ———
    5. Bring (from Copley II) tall stools for checkers   ———   ———

(h) Equipment
    1. Move bowling machine to 2nd floor   ———   ———
    2. Attempt to soften noise of cooler compressor or replace old coolers   ———   ———

(3) Tables—chairs
    NOTE: Present inventory includes benches—tables—the extra benches can

	Action Started	Action Completed

be used in pool room— 2nd floor _____ _____

(4) Purchase _____ new chairs for youth—drama, etc. programs _____ _____

(5) Purchase _____ new pedestal tables _____ _____

Refreshment Section:

Equipment (suggestions)
1. Refrigerator _____ _____
2. Potato Chip racks _____ _____
3. Hot Dog warmer _____ _____
4. Coin boxes _____ _____
5. Safe _____ _____
6. Cabinets—locked—for storage _____ _____
7. Soft drink machine _____ _____
8. _____ _____ _____
9. _____ _____ _____
10. _____ _____ _____

Supplies:
1. Soft drinks (source?) _____ _____
2. Candy—gum—etc., and rack (locked type) _____ _____
3. Coffee? _____ _____
4. Sandwich supply? _____ _____
5. Records for juke box _____ _____
6. _____ _____ _____
7. _____ _____ _____
8. _____ _____ _____
9. _____ _____ _____
10. _____ _____ _____

Staff—and control:
1. Director of program—paid _____ _____
2. Police protection—paid _____ _____
3. Phone in basement for emergencies _____ _____
4. Refreshment counter and roving control, 2 men—paid _____ _____
5. Checking system—1 teenager—paid _____ _____
6. _____ _____ _____
7. _____ _____ _____
8. _____ _____ _____
9. _____ _____ _____
10. _____ _____ _____

Action Action
Started Completed

Membership Section:
1. Age division 17 thru 20 _____ _____
2. Stag or couples—or both? _____ _____
3. Identification—methods:
  (a) By personal cards—(driver's
     license)
  (b) Sign-up sheets _____ _____
  (c) By membership cards _____ _____
    (1) Develop club card? _____ _____
    (2) Use picture identification? _____ _____
    (3) Source of developing card:
      a. Department _____ _____
      b. Commercial _____ _____
  (d) Nightly Exits–Entrance
    (1) None allowed _____ _____
    (2) If allowed—means of re-
      turning:
      a. Identification card _____ _____
      b. Tags _____ _____
      c. Listing of entry by
        means of names on
        roster _____ _____
      d. _____ _____ _____
      e. _____ _____ _____
4. Control Procedures:
  (a) Hours 8:00 (8:30) to 11:30
    (12:30) _____ _____
  (b) Day of week _____ _____ _____
    Weeks per month _____ _____ _____
  (c) Signs:
    (1) "No Drinking"–"No
      Gambling" _____ _____
    (2) Checking system _____ _____
    (3) Rules—Regulations _____ _____
    (4) Bulletin board _____ _____
    (5) Age limitations _____ _____
    (6) Dress—and behavior _____ _____
    (7) Exit or (no exit) privileges _____ _____
    (8) _____ _____ _____
    (9) _____ _____ _____
    (10) _____ _____ _____

	Action Started	Action Completed

Program Section:
1. Band:
   (a) Combo–3 or 4 pieces   ———   ———
   (b) Special singers–or performers   ———   ———
2. Juke Box   ———   ———
3. Guest performances:
   (a) Drama Guild   ———   ———
   (b) Special singing group (at special membership for cost)   ———   ———
4. Arrangements for out-of-club programs?   ———   ———
5. _____   ———   ———
6. _____   ———   ———
7. _____   ———   ———
8. _____   ———   ———
9. _____   ———   ———
10. _____   ———   ———

Finance Section:
1. Nightly fee cost per person
   75¢ $1.00 $1.25 $1.50   ———   ———
2. Capacity of room:
   150   300   500   ———   ———
   Estimate–nightly revenue
   $100.00 $150.00   etc.
3. Cost of repairing juke box   ———   ———
4. Cost of record supply   ———   ———
5. Cost of combo–band?
   $50.00
   $75.00
   $100.00
   $150.00   ———   ———
6. Salaries of control personnel
   (a) Director of club
       $2.25
       $2.50
       $ per hr.   ———   ———
   (b) Assistants
       (1) Refreshment counter and control
           $1.75 $2.00 $2.10
           $2.20 $ per hr.   ———   ———
       (2) Teenage checker
           $1.00 $1.25 $1.50
           $1.75 $ per hr.   ———   ———

Action   Action
Started   Completed

    (3) Police Control
        One Police (P.D.) at
        $ per hr.
        Two Police (P.D.) at
        $ per hr.   _____   _____
    (4) Other salaried help
    _____   _____   _____
    _____   _____   _____

    (5) Method of remuneration
        (a) Cash from nightly re-
           ceipts–
           by receipt
        (b) Check (from club
           account)
        (c) Check (from P.D.
           account)
           (d) Other _____
           (e) _____
           (f) _____   _____   _____
7. Estimate of current nightly oper-
    ating cost–using base estimates.
    NOTE: Building–heat janitor, etc.
        to be amortized in Recreation
        Budget
        Nightly   _____   _____
        (a) Membership (120 x atten-
           dance x $ =
        (b) Refreshments
           (?Est.   ) =
           Total   _____   _____
Expenses Nightly:
  1. Program Director
    $2.50 x 5 = $ x   hrs.
    $ (7:30–11:30 p.m.)
  2. Assistant–Adults (2)
    $ x 5 = $ x   hrs.
    $ (For refreshment control)   _____   _____
    (c) Checkers–$ x   =
        $
        Total leadership costs–
        estimated $ _____   _____
    (d) Protection–Police $
        Total personnel cost–
        estimated $ _____   _____

	Action Started	Action Completed
(e) Music–nightly $		
$ $ $		
(1) Orchestra $		
(f) Refreshments–		
reimbursable $		
TOTAL $		

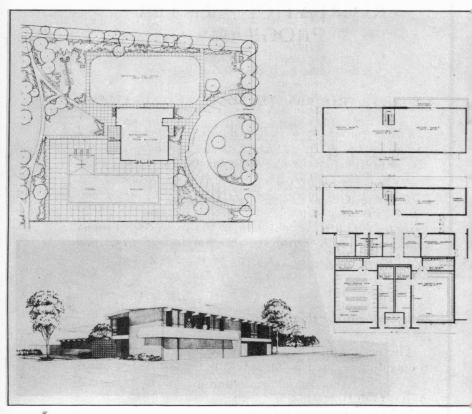

This recreation center provides ice skating and swimming in addition to meeting rooms.

6

RECREATION CENTER PROGRAMS

GENERAL PROGRAM FEATURES AND SERVICES

The activities carried on in recreation centers depend primarily upon the facilities in the building and the resourcefulness of the leaders in putting them to varied recreation use. Where the gymnasium is the chief feature, sports and games are likely to receive major emphasis. Social, cultural, and small group activities of various types are predominant in the programs at many smaller buildings. Buildings with ample and diversified facilities make possible a great variety of indoor recreation activities.

Programming for the School Recreation Center

The wide range of activities for which various schoolrooms may be used is suggested by the list which follows:

AUDITORIUM
1. Dramatic presentations
2. Symphony orchestra rehearsal

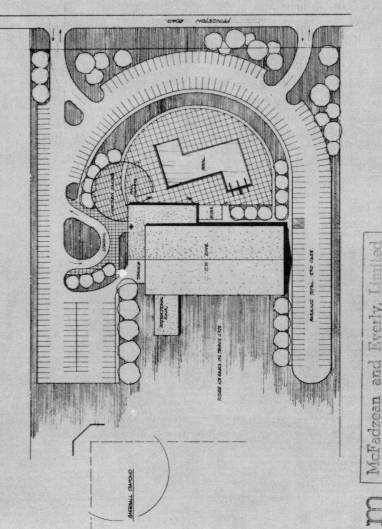

A complete change from a community center is this proposed covered ice skating rink and swimming pool.

3. Forums and lectures
4. Band concerts
5. Choral group rehearsal
6. Motion pictures
7. Dance band rehearsal
8. Minstrel
9. Recitals

LARGE GYMNASIUM
1. Exhibitions and demonstrations
2. Club activity program
3. Leagues in all sports
4. Special holiday dances
5. Game tournaments
6. Apparatus groups
7. Fencing groups
8. Scout programs
9. Boxing classes
10. Calisthenics

MEDICAL ROOM
1. Home nursing instruction
2. First-aid classes
3. Hygiene classes

CLASS ROOMS
1. Club meetings
2. Dressing rooms
3. Check rooms
4. Civic group meetings

MUSIC ROOM
1. Choral group rehearsals
2. Club meetings
3. Band rehearsals

SEWING ROOM
1. Handicraft groups
2. Parties and socials
3. Club meetings

SHOPS
1. Crafts, leather, wood, metal
2. Ceramics

COOKING ROOM
1. Nutrition classes
2. Preparation of party refreshments

Programming for the Municipal Recreation Center

Listed below are some of the more common types of recreation activities provided by municipal recreation departments through the promotion of an indoor center program:

ARTS AND CRAFTS
1. Applied arts—home decorations, gift articles, art novelties
2. Crocheting—laces, gloves, neckwear, scarfs, purses
3. Flower Making—woodfiber, paper, silk, organdie
4. Food preparation and service
5. Garment remodeling
6. Leather tooling—coin purses, handbags, book covers, novelties
7. Metal work—bowls, dishes, jewelry, book-ends, candlesticks, etc.
8. Painting—water color, oil
9. Pottery and clay making
10. Ceramics
11. Sculpture
12. Wood Carving

ATHLETICS AND SPORTS

1. Badminton—informal play and tournaments
2. Boxing—organized scientific instruction—pulleys, platform bag, shadow boxing, rope skipping, calisthenics, limited bouts.
3. Gymnasium classes—keeping fit classes for adults, reducing classes, and general gymnasium classes for adults
4. Low organized games—for boys and girls who do not care to participate in the highly organized team games
5. Table tennis—informal play, instruction, municipal leagues, and tournaments
6. Team games—The center gymnasium offers opportunity for informal games of basketball, and volleyball for both boys and girls and men and women. Those who desire membership in formally organized teams for local league play will find opportunity for such participation in municipal leagues. The regularly scheduled league games provide the general public with an opportunity to witness high-grade play in the various sports.

DANCING

1. Creative dancing
2. Married couple dance clubs
3. Golden Age dance clubs (Retired segment of the population)
4. Saturday evening informals
5. Teen-Age dances
6. Social dancing—special classes for high school groups and adults
7. Tap dancing

GAMES

1. Billiards—pocket billiards

2. Checkers—informal play, instruction, intersocial center league, municipal checker league for adults
3. Chess—informal play, instruction in beginners' and advanced classes at all centers, municipal tournaments and leagues, exhibition by masters
4. Contract bridge—classes in bidding and play of the hand
5. Table games—miniature bowling, parchesi, dominoes, rook, flinch, etc.

LITERARY
1. Debating clubs
2. Public speaking classes
3. Reading clubs

MUSIC
1. Bands
2. Glee clubs—men, women, or mixed group
3. Novelty bands
4. Opera clubs
5. Orchestras
6. Ukelele clubs
7. Vocal training classes

DRAMATICS
1. Social center drama clubs
2. Theatre parties
3. One act plays
4. Theatre workshops
5. Play reading groups

PHOTOGRAPHY
1. Advance classes—chemistry of photography, filters, and filter factors; enlargements, homemade equipment and darkrooms
2. Beginners' classes—parts, construction, and manipula-

tion of the camera; physics and chemistry of photography; developing and printing
3. Photographic art clubs
4. Photographic art shows
5. Photographic art clinics

CIVIC AND SOCIAL FEATURES
1. Boy scouts
2. Golden age clubs
3. Girl scouts
4. Teenage clubs
5. Mothers' clubs
6. Nursery school
7. Married people's social clubs

COMMUNITY FEATURES
1. Weekly entertainments—motion pictures, recitals, concerts, lectures, plays, etc.
2. Saturday open house for children and adults (afternoons)
3. Saturday night informals—dancing, table tennis, etc.

FORUMS
1. Lectures and discussion of topics of local and national interest
2. Special youth forums

TEEN-AGE PROGRAMS

Student Union

The Evanston, Illinois, Student Union is an excellent example of teen-agers' participation and efforts in providing themselves with a place to "hang out." Remember, this union's success has primarily depended on interested citizens and active youth.

SAMPLE UNION PROGRAM DEVELOPMENT

(The following material was used to conduct a fund drive)

The Evanston Student Union's building fund campaign is now in progress.

Local businessmen, members of community organizations and representatives of charitable foundations have been interested in the progress of this drive, and have asked that background material and general information be written for usage by their groups.

To this end a Student Union Committee has compiled and edited the following brochure, designed to be of assistance to groups wishing to participate in the financial program of the Union:

OUTLINE

1. What is the Evanston Student Union?
2. Background of the Evanston Student Union movement.
3. Present program and future expectations.
4. Financing the student union.
5. Summary of contributory projects.
6. An appeal from the Student Union Board.
7. A resolution from the City of Evanston.

WHAT IS THE EVANSTON STUDENT UNION

The Evanston Student Union is the "New Scene" of activity for high school age persons. It is a union of students, managed by students, for service to all the high school students in the City of Evanston. Its new building will be a meeting place for entertainment, for dancing, for music and drama, for games and relaxation, for eating and conversation; and also for sharing and working together, and for community service.

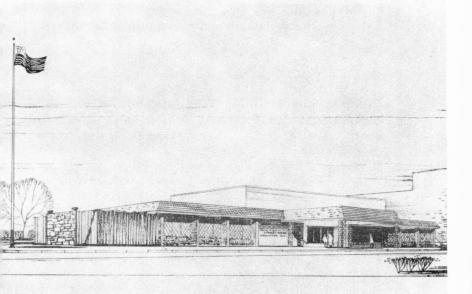

JOSEPH + SARAH LEVY
STUDENT UNION
EVANSTON, ILLINOIS

Teen centers are becoming popular. Specific maintenance situations are created when a teen group decorates a brand-new teen center.

The Evanston Student Union is also a practical reality; an environment in which a planned and supervised program of social, recreational, educational, and healthful development can be fostered . . . to the enrichment of the entire community.

HOWEVER, the Evanston Student Union is not just a building and a program. It is also a working philosophy of unity and service existing in the minds of its members. This is evidenced by their efforts to work together to serve all elements of Evanston's high school population and also by their acceptance of the responsibility for raising a share of the money necessary to equip their building.

YOU ARE WELCOME

to participate in the experience and the spirit of the Evanston Student Union. Please read further to look into the background of this unique project, and to discover how your group or organization may share in the future of its program.

THE EVANSTON STUDENT UNION: EARLY HISTORY

Youth Commission

The creation of the Evanston Youth Commission in 1965 made possible a continuation of a community-wide evaluation of the unmet needs of young people, originally begun by the Mayor's temporary study group. Through the efforts of the Commission steps were made to inform the public, to expand services already being rendered, and to develop new services which could be extended throughout all segments of the community.

Part of the Commission's fact-finding program was conducted in homerooms at Evanston Township High School, using surveys and informal meetings with students. From this first hand communication with students came the realization that perhaps the students themselves were best qualified to develop and foster experimental programs and activities for people in their own age group.

Student Development Group

Throughout 1965 an ad hoc committee of ETHS students, Youth Commission Members, representatives from the City Council, and members of the Parks and Recreation Department met to discuss the students' needs and how these needs might be met.

A City-Wide student nucleus group representing ETHS, St. George, Marywood, and Roycemore was formed in February of 1966 and chose for itself the name "EVANSTON STUDENT UNION." This pilot coordinating committee recommended the sponsorship of social activities that would bring together students from the entire community and asked that an Adult Advisory Group be formed to work with them toward this end.

Early Programs Established

With the cooperation of City Officials, and under the guidance of the Department of Parks and Recreation, a series of Saturday night dances at a community center was scheduled. A staff member from the Recreation Department was assigned to work with the students and their Adult Advisory Board.

From this came the creation of "THE SCENE," a "Night Club" type meeting place for all high school teens, and a common meeting ground for the sharing of responsibility for planning, organizing, financing, and conducting programs and activities of the Evanston Student Union.

Plans for a permanent organization grew. In the spring representative elections for additional committee members were conducted and a membership program for the "SCENE" began. At graduation time the first regular election of officers was held, and the Board of Directors of the Evanston Student Union was established.

THE PRESENT

With the establishment of formal leadership represented by its Board, the Evanston Student Union planned a variety of summer activities and programs that would appeal to wider interests, such as special events, beach parties, new dance locations, and, of course, a continuation of "THE SCENE."

In order to enable the new Union to raise funds for its

activities the Adult Advisory Board formed a non-profit corporation, "THE EVANSTON STUDENT UNION, INC.," whose charter was granted by the State of Illinois at the close of the summer.

What is significant in the name of the new corporation is the word "UNION," truly representative of all the hopes and goals of the original nucleus group whose primary purpose was to further and develop community unity among all students.

AND THE FUTURE

The program of the Evanston Student Union had been witnessed by Mr. Joseph Levy.

His involvement with the Evanston Student Union had been stimulated by seeing that these young people possessed the ability to develop for themselves a program that was marked by maturity and progressiveness. This was the type of program that deserved the kind of permanence that could be provided only in the form of mortar, brick, and stone.

His donation to the City of Evanston of such a building, dedicated to the future of Evanston's youth, thereby established such permanence.

FINANCING THE EVANSTON STUDENT UNION

1. The Joseph and Sarah Levy Family Foundation has made a gift of $175,000 to the City of Evanston for the purpose of constructing the Student Union building.
2. The City of Evanston has provided the land upon which the Union is being constructed. The site is located at 1700 Maple Avenue, and is valued at $85,000.
3. The City of Evanston has guaranteed the provision of any extra construction costs as necessary. It is now estimated that additional costs will amount to $42,000.
4. The Student members themselves will be financially responsible for raising money to cover costs of annual

program expenses, provision of program supplies, repair and replacement of equipment, and similar annual expenses. They plan to raise this money by

    a. Sale of memberships

    b. Admission charges to dances

    c. Food services operation

    d. Sponsorship of special events, shows and entertainments.

5. To insure continuation of the project the City will maintain the program of the Evanston Student Union for a minimum of 20 years under the auspices of the Playground and Recreation Board and will provide such funds as necessary to fulfill this purpose.

6. The students have also accepted the responsibility for certain capital expenditures needed to equip the building. These costs amount to $12,000 and include: interior decorations, furniture and furnishings, and permanent equipment. Their programs for community-wide fund raising activities to meet this $12,000 goal is as follows:

    a. Door-to-door solicitation campaign. This was conducted in July and August of 1966.

    b. Mailout campaign to parents of high school students. To be conducted in the Fall of 1966.

    c. Sales campaign co-sponsored as a joint project with the Evanston Lions Club. To be conducted in December of 1966.

    d. Participation from service clubs, business firms, community organizations, and charitable foundations. In progress at present time.

PARTICIPATION FROM COMMUNITY ORGANIZATIONS

The Evanston City Council has made an official proclamation of invitation and encouragement to all "Individuals, Businesses and Philanthropic Foundations" for participation in the financial support of the Evanston Student Union.

The following cost summary illustrates some of the out-standing needs that must be met, arranged in the form of suggested projects for the consideration of groups and organizations:

Program Facility Projects

Kitchen	$3,296.00
Stove	250.00
Counter Table	125.00
Freezer	200.00
Soda Bar	1,800.00
Refrigerator	250.00
Popcorn Maker	199.00
Expresso Machine	90.00
Pizza Oven	115.00
Hot Dog Steamer	68.00
Deep Fryer	99.00
Utensils	100.00
Ice Cream Freezer	NC
Coffee House	$2,969.49
Furniture	2,669.49
Folding Stage	300.00
Conference	
Lounge	$1,578.99
Furniture	1,578.99

Building Equipment Projects

Office	$990.00
Desk	177.00
3 Chairs	137.00
Typewriter	190.00
Mimeo	300.00
3 Cabinets	186.00
Cloak Room	$2,684.00
Coat-Racks for 1M @ 1.25 Lin. Feet	2,500.00
Checks	90.00
Tables	94.00

Stage	$1,800.00
Draperies and Curtains	1,500.00
Lighting	300.00
Game Room	$1,404.40
2 Pool Tables	898.00
Bumper Pool	129.00
2 Table Tennis	260.00
Cabinet	87.40
Supplies	30.00
Miscellaneous Projects	$4,570.00
Juke Box	800.00
Piano	450.00
PA System	2,000.00
Phonograph	350.00
Movie Projector	490.00
Stage Screen	180.00
TV	300.00
Auditorium	$6,708.00
600 Chairs	4,800.00
12 Chair Trucks	936.00
12 - 8″ Tables	564.00
4 - 12″ Tables	408.00

AN OPEN LETTER FROM OFFICERS OF THE
EVANSTON STUDENT UNION, INC.

We are asking for financial assistance from groups, organizations and foundations to help us successfully meet the opening date deadline of the new Student Union building in December of 1966. In order to better explain our program to your own group, we would appreciate the opportunity of having our student delegates visit you in person, for the purpose of presenting our message to you by means of a verbal presentation.

MAY WE HEAR FROM YOU SOON?

Thank you very much for your interest and support in the Evanston Student Union.

HOW YOU CAN HELP IN THE MANAGEMENT OF THE UNION

Student members themselves manage and operate the Evanston Student Union, through participation in a variety of important volunteer work committees. It is expected of each member that he or she will share in the work load of making the Union a success.

Please check your volunteer work choices below, and indicate how many hours per month you will be available for service.

....Program Planning
....Finance and Purchasing
....Publicity
....Fund Drive Campaign
....Decorations and Lighting
....Clean up Committee
....Rules and Regulations
....Entertainment and Dances
....Snack bar
....Host or Hostess
....Membership recruitment
....Checkroom
....Admissions gate
....Other Ideas (Please list) :

Please add your suggestions for improved programs and facilities:

THE EVANSTON STUDENT UNION

The Evanston Student Union is a new concept of planning, organizing and conducting of leisure time activities for all high school students in the City of Evanston.

It is new because activities and programs are sponsored by the students themselves, through their elected Board of officers which represent all high schools in the City.

VARIETY OF ACTIVITIES

Most activities are just plain fun: Parties, dances, top bands, relaxation, meeting new friends, and: using the Union as a gathering place on weekend evenings and during after-school hours.

Activities also include talent shows, clubs, special interest groups, entertainment, tournaments, and fundraising.

Much of the program is involved in service to others; working on volunteer committees, operating the game room, checkroom and coffee house, and also providing assistance in community service projects.

PROGRAM SCHEDULES

The Union is open every day after school and on Saturday evenings. Special events are planned for selected Friday nights and Saturday afternoons. During the summer months the Union is open on two additional nights every week.

BECOMING A MEMBER

All participants must be registered as a member in good standing of the Evanston Student Union. Details on joining the Evanston Student Union are found inside.

THE LEVY FOUNDATION

This outstanding building was donated to the City of Evanston by the Joseph and Sarah Levy Family Foundation, as a dedication to all high school students.

Planning and design of the facilities was provided by student members of the Board of the Student Union, with the guidance of their adult advisory board.

MAGNIFICENT FACILITIES INCLUDE:

. . . Large stage and auditorium area, accommodating 800 for dancing or 600 seated for stage performances.

. . . English style Coffee House which seats 64. The kitchen is maintained by a licensed catering firm and the menu is designed by the members. In the Coffee House special entertainment programs are presented also.

. . . Lounge provides another place for refreshments and relaxation, and is also used for TV watching, meetings of small groups, and conferences.

. . . Well equipped Game Room for pool, table tennis, and other games.

. . . Outdoor enclosed Patio used in warm weather. Coffee House menu available also.

. . . Other facilities include membership and program offices, backstage dressing rooms and storage, and a checkroom accommodating 1000 persons.

ADULT SUPERVISION

Supervision from adults is provided by staff from the Department of Parks and Recreation, from off-duty police officers, and from volunteer chaperones representing community organizations. The Adult Advisory Board serves as the corporate board of governors.

STUDENT UNION
MEMBERSHIP APPLICATION
RULES & REGULATIONS

1. Membership in the Evanston Student Union is open to all students who attend a high school in the City of Evanston, and to residents of Evanston who attend

a high school elsewhere.

2. The Membership fee is $5.00 per year, payable October 1 of each year. Split year payment plan is available.

3. A member may bring a single guest on a "one at a time" basis. All guests must be registered on a guest pass in advance of the activity. The sponsoring member is responsible for the conduct, behavior and transportation of the guest.

4. Persons who are eligible for membership in the Evanston Student Union may be a guest for one activity only. Thereafter, such persons must take out a regular membership in the Student Union.

5. Proof of identification is required of all members and guests.

6. The Student Union Board is empowered to enforce all rules and regulations and to advise and counsel individuals with regard to attitude, manner and behavior. In addition the Board will enforce a "Code of Conduct" which recommends proper habits of dress, dancing, amorous behavior, reputation, maturity, etc.

7. It shall be understood by all participants that behavior and conduct will be maintained at a high level. Persons whose conduct does not meet the approval of the Student Union Board are subject to removal from the premises, suspension of privileges or possible forfeiture of the membership card.

8. Persons who are suspected of having indulged in alcoholic beverages will be refused admission to the program.

9. All participants are expected to maintain cleanliness and orderliness of the facilities at all times. Members ar expected to assist periodically in the work of volunteer service committees.

10. Loitering on the exterior of the building or on adjacent city streets is prohibited. The Board will take

disciplinary action in cases of misconduct that occur enroute to or from home to the Student Union.

All participants should familiarize themselves with any other regulations that exist at the Union concerning use of game room, lounge, and coffee house facilities.

Please cut here and mail or bring in application with membership fee to:

EVANSTON STUDENT UNION,
c/o DEPARTMENT OF PARKS and RECREATION
1802 MAPLE AVENUE, EVANSTON, ILLINOIS
(Fill out reverse side)

EVANSTON STUDENT UNION
MEMBERSHIP APPLICATION
Please print:

NAME _____

ADDRESS _____PHONE _____

SCHOOL _____GRADE _____

PARENT'S NAME _____

Fee Enclosed: $5.00 to October 1.

I do hereby agree to uphold the rules and regulations of the Evanston Student Union. I realize that failure to do so will result in suspension of privileges and possible forfeiting of membership:

_____   _____
signature   date

SUPER SUMMER NEWSLETTER

SUPER SUMMER SCHEDULE OPENS WITH "MAID MOD SHOW AND DANCE"

IT'S HIP, GROOVY, BOSS, AND MAD . . . . THE "MAD MOD" SHOW AND DANCE OPENING SUPER SUMMER WEDNESDAY, JUNE 21

Fashions by MALE M-1 Shop of Pipers Alley, Old Town! Models from ESU Fashion Board members. Dancing to a famous Old Town Combo. Super opening for Super Summer!

SUMMER EVENING SCHEDULE

ESU open every:
WEDNESDAY — 8 to 10:30 P.M.
FRIDAY   — 8 to 11:00 P.M.
SATURDAY   — 8 to 11:30 P.M.

WATCH FOR SPECIAL AFTERNOON SCHEDULES!

WORLD TEENAGE SHOW:
NAVY PIER
A HAPPENING!

See the Student Union Booth Tuesday, June 27 at this fabulous show! Want a special ESU bus trip? Consult an ESU Board member.

TOP TALENT WANTED:
IT'S SHOWTIME

Can you sing, dance, act, etc. Do you want professional coaching in production? Sign up for ESU's first annual summer the-

BAND BATTLE
FRIDAY AUDITION
Friday, June 23:
NEW SOCIETY
VS
THE THYME

MEMBERSHIP PROGRAM HIGHLIGHTS

NEEDED: 500 new members for a super summer! Fee: $2.50, good until October 1, 1973. Seniors please take notice! SPECIAL OFFER: Free membership for next year to all persons who can sell 20 memberships by July 15.

SPECIAL EVENTS
HIGHLIGHT
ESU's SUPER SUMMER

Bus trips to Ravinia: SEE THE ASSOCIATION: PETER NERO DUKE ELLINGTON

to run throughout the summer. Showtime production in August.

LEARN JAZZ AND ROCK THIS SUMMER

Gain proficiency in jazz and rock music with the ESU's individual and group instruction program. Guidance from professional music groups, combos and musicians. "INSTANT ROCK" BY THE Sidewinders!

SATURDAY NITE DANCE SCHEDULE

Clip this out and save:
June 10 – PRIDE AND JOY
June 17 – REVELLES
June 24 – MAUDS
July 1 – DUTCH MASTERS
July 8 – GROUPE
July 15 – FIVE BUCKS
July 22 – CHANGING TIMES
July 29 – CHICAGO SONICS

VOLUNTEER WORKERS WANTED

Your Student Union Board is seeking more managers to operate the Student Union. Please sign up at the office.

TWENTY-FIVE MODELS NEEDED FOR THE ANNUAL FALL FASHION SHOW: 10 boys and 15 girls needed for Fashion Board this summer. Fall Fashion show cosponsored by SAKS FIFTH AVE—August 11!

SPORTS CAR RALLYE
DRAG RACE TRIP

Ski Club and Car Club Films throughout the summer!

FREE COKES IN THE COFFEE HOUSE

Bring the envelope this newsletter came in: It's worth one free coke!

BEACH BLAST COMING JUNE 30

First Beach Party for your super summer now scheduled for Dempster Street Beach: Friday, June 30, Time 7–11 P.M.
LIVE COMBO . . . EATS . . . SWIMMING

NEED PAID SUMMER EMPLOYMENT?

Register with the Student Union office for:
PART TIME EMPLOYMENT
FULL TIME EMPLOYMENT
Co-Sponsor: Evanston Youth Commission and Employment Bureau.

Teen-Age Rules

> *Youth behavior rules presented here were developed by over ten adult organizations in a suburban town. The wider the support of adult and youth behavior guidelines, the greater the guidelines' acceptance. Your knowledge of the youth and their level of community social activities should help you in developing your recreation center's behavior rules.*

STATEMENT OF PRINCIPLE

A number of parents have been disturbed by the acceleration of social activities which have brought adult activities into high school age level and high school age activities into the grade school age level. This acceleration has hampered the complete development of the child and had frequently brought premature sophistication and its many accompanying problems.

Additionally, school and civic groups as well as individual parents are concerned when young people get into difficulties.

Therefore, a need has been felt for a list of recommendations for parents of teen-agers. This outline, prepared and endorsed by a large number of organizations, contains a list of parental responsibilities and an outline of recommended regulations for teen-agers.

The principles underlying these recommendations should not supersede those of the individual family. A set of principles established and adhered to by a group of parents can reinforce the standards of the family. It is a far easier task to abide by our beliefs if there are others who believe as we do. It is our hope that this list will help responsible parents answer the "everyone else does" argument effectively.

1. Parents must assume the responsibility for setting limits on their teen-agers.

2. Parents should treat each teen-ager with dignity and consideration, allowing him to participate in some family decisions.

3. Parents should make and enforce the rules consistently.

4. Increased privileges should be granted as young people demonstrate the ability to assume greater responsibility.

5. It is the parent's duty to know where their young people are and with whom they associate. Parents should know what their young people are doing and what time they will return home.

6. Parents should make sure their young people know how and where to reach them at all times.

7. Parents should stimulate their young people's interest in the knowledge of God and religion by taking an active part in their Church or Synagogue. Human dignity should be stressed.

8. Parents should teach respect for the law by example.

DATING

1. Parents should discourage car dates, where the sole purpose is to ride around with no specific destination or other activity planned.

2. Parents should discourage dating until ninth grade at the earliest.

3. Single-dating is not recommended until the Junior and Senior year of high school.

4. Steady dating should be discouraged for high school students with the possible exception of seniors. Steady dating means: (1) Frequent (once a week or more often) and exclusive dating of one boy and one girl; (2) Promises to each other that they will date no one else; (3) Acceptance on the part of their friends that they are to be dated by no one else.

Funds from public tax and private donations provided Sterling, Illinois, with this excellent recreation facility.

5. Young people should be taught at an early age that steady dating could be a serious step toward marriage.

6. Parents must explain clearly to teen-agers the hour at which they are expected home.

ACTIVITIES

1. Social activities are not recommended on school nights.

2. Going downtown at night without an adult is unwise, at least before the eleventh grade.

3. Parents are wise to stress the home as the primary center of recreation where the whole family may share in it.

4. It is generally advisable for boys and girls to stay within their own age groups.

5. Teen-agers should be encouraged to bring their friends into their home; however, a parent must be

at home if a teen-ager is entertaining a date or friends.

6. Invitations to parties should be sent out, and should clearly state the date and the exact hours. Parents should see that the party ends on schedule and that those attending have direct transportation to their homes.

7. Parents should not allow party-crashers and should not permit their teen-agers to be party-crashers. In the event a party is crashed by uninvited teen-agers, they should be asked firmly to leave. If they refuse, their parents should be contacted. Open house parties should be discouraged owing to the fact that groups of youngsters too large to control may be attracted. They are often stepping stones to problems at other locations.

8. Boys and girls attending social functions on a no-date basis should have parent transportation both to and from the affair.

9. With a few exceptions (in regard to school work, etc.) it is poor taste for a girl to telephone a boy.

10. Drive-in theatre dates should not be permitted.

11. Parents should check closely on teen regulations at a household where his teen-ager is spending the night.

12. Parents should be sure the motion picture their teen-agers are to attend is consistent with the parents' moral objectives. Parents can refer to their religious publications or national magazines such as *Parents,* P.T.A. magazines, or other publications for their recommendations, or rely on the movie industry's rating system.

13. Parents should discourage all frequenting of public, unsupervised areas after dark.

DRESS

1. Teen-agers should be encouraged to be neat and tidy. They should attend all affairs dressed appropriately.

2. Parents of teen-age girls should guide their daughters to use make-up and choose hair styles appropriate to their age.
3. Overly brief or revealing attire should be discouraged.

DRIVING

1. Parents should permit a teen to drive only if he has a valid license.
2. When the privilege of driving a car is abused, it should be withdrawn.
3. Parents should not permit sons or daughters to drive recklessly or ride with reckless drivers.
4. Parents should know and obey all laws governing the use of motor vehicles and should encourage their teen-agers by observing regulations and rules themselves.
5. Parents should encourage their teen-ager to complete a driver education course.
6. The actual miles covered by a teen-ager while driving should be in consonance with the distance authorized by his parents.

DRINKING AND SMOKING

1. Parents must prohibit teen-age drinking. Should an alcoholic beverage be brought to a teen-age party in the home, it should be impounded and the parents of the offender notified.
2. Parents should disapprove of teen-agers smoking and should remind their young people that smoking in public and the purchase of cigarettes is unlawful in the State of Illinois for youngsters under 18 years of age. (Again, each state has its own age limit.)

DRUG ABUSE

It is important that recreators and parents recognize the common symptoms and signs of drug abuse, since many potential hard-core addicts can be rehabilitated if their involvement in drug abuse is detected in its early stages.

1. Common symptoms of drug abuse:
   a. Changes in school attendance, discipline and grades.
   b. Change in the character of homework turned in.
   c. Unusual flare-ups or outbreaks of temper.
   d. Poor physical appearance.
   e. Furtive behavior regarding drugs and possessions.
   f. Wearing of sunglasses at inappropriate times to hide dilated or constricted pupils.
   g. Long-sleeved shirts worn constantly to hide needle marks.
   h. Association with known drug abusers.
   i. Borrowing of money from students to purchase drugs.
   j. Stealing small items from school.
   k. Finding the student in odd places during the day—such as closets, storage rooms, etc.—to take drugs.
2. Manifestations of specific drugs:
   a. The glue sniffer.
      i. Odor of substance inhaled on breath and clothes.
      ii. Excess nasal secretions, watering of the eyes.
      iii. Poor muscular control, drowsiness or unconsciousness.
      iv. Presence of plastic or paper bags or rags containing dry plastic cement.
   b. The depressant abuser (barbiturates, "goofballs," "downers") :
      i. Symptoms of alcohol intoxication with one important exception—no odor of alcohol on the breath.
      ii. Staggering or stumbling in classrooms or halls.
      iii. May fall asleep in activity.
      iv. Lacks interest in recreational center activities.
      v. Is drowsy and may appear disoriented.

Barbiturates are manufactured depressant drugs which

are administered for the purpose of relaxing the central nervous system. There are about 400 varieties of barbiturates on the market but the ones in greatest use are phenobarbital (nembutal), secobartiol (seconal), amobarbital (amytal), butabarbital (butisol) and tuinal. The slang terms are "goof balls," "barbs," "red birds," "yellow jackets," "red Devils," "trees" or "Xmas trees," "blue heavens," "nimby" and "seccy."

Barbiturates are considered to be highly dangerous when taken without medical supervision. They are known to slow down the heart rate, lower blood pressure, slow down reactions and responses, produce drowsiness and deep sleep. High doses cause one to be confused, have slurred speech; ability to think, to concentrate and to work is greatly reduced. Abusers of these drugs become irritable, tend to fight and are abusive. Their emotional threshold is lowered so that they are unpredictable.

Barbiturates are physically and psychologically addicting—that is, the body needs increasing amounts to produce the desired effect. Withdrawal from "barbs" takes longer and is more dangerous than that of the opiate abusers. Abrupt withdrawal may result in convulsion and possibly death. Mixing of barbiturates and alcohol may cause death.

    c. The stimulant abuser (amphetamines, "uppers," "bennies," "speed") :

        i. Excess activity: student is irritable, argumentative, nervous, and has difficulty sitting still in classrooms.

       ii. Pupils are dilated.

     iii. Mouth and nose are dry with bad breath, causing user to lick his lips frequently and rub and scratch his nose.

     iv. Chain smoking.

      v. User goes long periods without eating or sleeping.

d. The narcotic abuser (heroin, demerol, morphine, etc.) :

These individuals are not frequently seen in school or recreation centers and usually begin by drinking paregoric or cough medicines containing codeine. The presence of empty bottles in wastebaskets or on school grounds is a clue.

   i. Inhaling ("snorting") heroin in powder form leaves traces of white powder around the nostrils, causing redness and rawness.

   ii. Injecting ("mainlining") heroin leaves scars on the inner surface of the arms and elbows. This causes the user to wear long-sleeved shirts most of the time.

   iii. Users often leave syringes, bent spoons, cotton and needles in lockers: this is the telltale sign of an addict.

   iv. In the classroom the pupil is lethargic, drowsy. His pupils are constricted and fail to respond to light.

THE OPIATES:

Opium is extracted from the poppy plant. This dark gummy substance is the base for the different opiates and their compounds: codeine, dilaudid, laudanum, metopon, oxycodone, pantapon, paregoric, percodan, morphine, and heroin. The two synthetic opiates are demerol (meperidine) and dolophine (methadone). The two most widely abused opiates are morphine and heroin.

Morphine, a bitter, white, odorless powder is a pain killer and is a valuable drug when used under medical supervision. The slang term is "M" or "Monkey" and "White stuff." Morphine may be taken in capsule form but the addict usually "mainlines" it—injects it directly into a vein.

Morphine is an addicting drug which is not so popular as heroin because pushers find it less profitable.

Heroin (diacetylmorphine) is a derivative of morphine, a white odorless powder which is stronger than morphine and therefore more addicting. The slang terms for heroin are "H," "horse," "boy," "junk," "white stuff," "big Harry," "smack," and also "cabello."

Heroin is sold in capsules ("caps") or in paper envelopes ("decks"). Heroin may be taken orally, sniffed or injected into the veins. Since it acts more quickly when injected, this method is most commonly used. Users of heroin become physically and psychologically addicted very quickly. Since the drug is illegal in our country, it is purchased on the black market, which may mean that a user may spend anywhere from $40.00 to $50.00 per day to maintain his habit. An overdose of heroin will cause unconsciousness or death.

  e. The marijuana abuser:

   They are difficult to recognize unless under the influence of the drug at the time they are being observed.

   i. In the early stages the user may appear animated and hysterical with rapid, loud talking and bursts of laughter.

   ii. In the later stages the user is sleepy or stuporous.

   iii. Depth perception is distorted, making driving dangerous.

   NOTE: Marijuana *(cannabis sativa)*, popularly known as "pot," "grass," "tea," "weed," "Mary Jane," is made of the leaves and flowering tops of the hemp plant. The leaves and flowering tops of the plant are dried, crushed or pulverized ("manicured") so that in appearance and texture it resembles oregano. Marijuana can be sniffed, chewed, brewed into tea, smoked in a pipe, or hand-rolled into a cigarette. The cigarette is the most popular form and is known as a "reefer," "stick," "Texas tea," "pot," "rope," "Mary Jane," "loco weed," "jive," "grass," "hemp," "hay." These cigarettes are rolled in a double thickness of brown or off-white cigarette paper. They are smaller than a regular cigarette, and the paper is twisted or tucked in at both ends. The "tobacco" is greener in color. The aroma of the cigarette is easily detected because it is rather heavy and sweetish.

f. The hallucinogen abuser:

It is unlikely that students who use LSD will do so in a school or recreational center setting since these drugs are usually used in a group situation under special conditions.

i. Users sit or recline quietly in a dream or trance-like state.

ii. Users may become fearful and experience a degree of terror which makes them attempt to escape from the group.

iii. The drug primarily affects the central nervous system, producing changes in mood and behavior.

iv. Perceptual changes involve sense of sight, hearing, touch, body-image and time.

NOTE: The drug is odorless, tasteless and colorless and may be found in the form of impregnated sugar cubes, cookies or crackers. LSD is usually taken orally but may be injected. Is imported in ampules of clear blue liquid.

SUGGESTIONS FOR SIXTH GRADERS

1. Hours: school nights 9 P.M., weekends 9:30 P.M. Boys and girls should not be allowed out after dark unless parents provide transportation to and from the activity.

2. Activities to be emphasized at this level are sports and recreation, scouts, music lessons, church groups.

Informal afternoon parties are to be preferred to night parties. The group idea should be emphasized at all social occasions, where both boys and girls are present. They should not date. It is suggested that the numbers be unequal.

SUGGESTIONS FOR SEVENTH AND EIGHTH GRADERS

1. Hours, school nights: 9:30 P.M., weekends 10:00 P.M. Boys and girls should not be allowed out after dark unless parents provide transportation to and from the activity.
2. Scouting, park district, YMCA, church groups, etc., programs offer a great deal to this age group.
3. Square dancing, family cook-outs are appropriate entertainment.
4. Instruction in ballroom dancing could begin at this age. Dances should be under the YMCA, or professional dance agency (co-sponsored by a school or community recreation agency.) Dancing could be more frequent in the eighth grade than the seventh.
5. Evening parties should be very infrequent.

SUGGESTIONS FOR FRESHMEN

1. Hours, school nights 9:45 P.M., weekends 10:15 P.M., supervised weekend activities 11:00 P.M.
2. Activities other than social should continue to be encouraged in order to keep proper balance.
3. A party should be an infrequent, special occasion.
4. This is the earliest year in which dating should begin. Single dating is premature. Double-dating or group get-togethers are preferred.

SUGGESTIONS FOR SOPHOMORES, JUNIORS AND SENIORS

1. Hours: 10:00 P.M. school nights, 11:30 P.M. week-

ends; 12:00 midnight on special occasions only.

2. Continue to guard against the overbalance of social life, to the exclusion of academic, cultural, and athletic activities.

3. Encourage the wholesomeness of many friendships by planning some group affairs where dating is not a requirement.

4. Parents should discourage teen-agers from "hanging-around" or loitering in public places or commercial recreation facilities.

YOUNG PEOPLE'S BILL OF RIGHTS

Regardless of Race, Color or Creed . . . The Right for Me to Have:

1. The affection and guidance of understanding parents.

2. A decent home in which I may be adequately fed, clothed, and sheltered.

3. Morality guidance and training.

4. A school program which offers me opportunity for development to my full potential.

5. Constructive discipline for the development of good character, conduct and habits.

6. Security in my community against influences detrimental to proper development.

7. The individual selection of wholesome recreation.

8. Life in a community in which the well-being of children is considered of primary importance.

9. Good adult example.

10. An opportunity for a job for my ability, training, and experience.

11. Protection against physical or moral employment hazards which make wholesome development difficult.

12. Health services to prevent and treat disease and to permit my mental, physical, and social development.

YOUNG PEOPLE'S BILL OF RESPONSIBILITIES

To God, My Country, My Parents and Myself That I May:

1. Grow in character and ability as I grow in size.
2. Be honest with myself and others in what I say and do.
3. Learn and practice my religion.
4. Honor my parents, my elders and my teachers.
5. Develop high moral principles and the courage to live by them.
6. Take good care of my body, mind, and spirit.
7. Respect the rights of others.
8. Set a good example so that others may enjoy and profit by my company.
9. Perform my work to the best of my ability.
10. Regard my education as a preparation for the future.
11. Obey our laws so that I may live in harmony with others.
12. Preserve and support our American way of life and government.

SENIOR CITIZENS PROGRAMS

Special Considerations

THE GOLDEN AGE CLUB PROGRAM

The general acceptance of the retirement age as sixty-five, and the increasing longevity of both men and women have created in every community a large group of chronologically aging citizens whose lives are no longer filled with the urgencies of making a living and raising a family. Many of these are unable to find a home with children or relatives and live alone. At the same time, experience has taught us that calendar years are no measure of age—all of us know "old folks" who are alert and physically active at seventy; we also know people who are old in interests and in physique at fifty. Communities have come to recognize that the later years of life can have a vital philosophy and momentum all their own, that they can combine the mellowness of years of living with new realms of experience—making new friends, finding companionship, discovering new social and recreational interests, uncovering hidden or forgotten skills and talents, and finding new ways to again become an integral part of the community.

PURPOSE OF THE PROGRAM

The primary objective of a recreation department in developing a Golden Age Club Program is to make available to the senior citizens of a community all the general recreational resources (social, cultural, creative) that can be adapted to their special needs and circumstances. The eminent psychiatrist, Dr. William Menninger, has stated that, "Recreation is an extremely important aid to growing active interest that provides satisfaction through participation. The elderly person with a hobby is almost always an alert, interesting person. By contrast, there is no more pathetic sight than the older person who has no interest in life and only sits and waits—vivid evidence of the value of recreation to mental health. We do not cease playing because we are old; we grow old because we cease playing."

To club members, a Golden Age Club offers insurance against loneliness through fellowship that may ripen into friendship and the security of belonging to a group that has status and in many instances substitutes for the family; the opportunity to maintain or renew self-respect through the recognition of one's fellow members; the opportunity to learn ways of improving one's health and living conditions; and the realization that one has still a significant voice in the affairs of the community and the nation.

To the leader, the club offers the challenge of guiding the members to the realization of all these opportunities.

However, in addition to achieving all the direct benefits of participation in recreational activities for the senior citizen, the recreation department also aims to create opportunities for service, social adjustment, and social development in order that the older person may lead a happy and meaningful life. The Golden Age Clubs and the All-City Golden Age Club Council are the organizational instruments through which these objectives are pursued.

GOLDEN AGE CLUBS

A Golden Age Club is many things to many people.

Structurally, the club is a very simple organization. Its members should come from all parts of the city, but more likely from the surrounding neighborhood, in response to the invitation of a friend, the suggestion of a neighbor, a public announcement in the newspaper, a leaflet carried into the home from school by a grandchild, or the recommendation of a social worker. All clubs should be open to men and women sixty years of age and over. Each club should have a greatly diversified cross-section of members with widely varied backgrounds—housewives, executives, policemen, firemen, plumbers, clerks, secretaries, school teachers, etc. Membership should be limited to fifty, and membership cards are issued for identification purposes. For further identification, an attractive small club pin may be obtained at a nominal fee. A member should belong to one club only.

Each club should have a professionally trained leader who carries the primary responsibility for organization and program, but whose work may gradually be lessened as the group draws up a simple constitution, elects officers, and appoints working committees that take over to a greater or lesser degree the responsibilities of program planning, arrangements, membership, etc.

A typical meeting consists of informal visiting and a community sing, followed by the introduction of guests, the announcement of birthdays, and the presentation of new members. Committee reports are given, special announcements are made, correspondence is read, and new business is then in order. Usually a social hour of cards or other games is held, or a special program presented, such as music, a dramatic skit, movies, or a speaker which is sometimes followed by a lively discussion. Refreshments of coffee and cake generally conclude the evening. A small box on the table invites voluntary contributions, which in most cases are sufficient to pay for the club's refreshments, to purchase greeting and special message cards, and to defray other miscellaneous expenses. This gives the members a feeling of independence and self-sufficiency. There is no membership fee.

THE ALL-CITY COUNCIL

The All-City Council is composed of two representatives from each of the Golden Age Clubs. This council serves as a planning and steering committee and does most of the coordinating for the all-city activities, such as picnics, bus trips, concerts, card tournaments, hobby shows, entertainments, and other program possibilities of a city-wide nature. The council meets regularly once a month. The director of the program, and often several club leaders are on hand to assist. Officers include a president, vice-president, and two secretaries (recording and corresponding) who are elected annually. The council is guided in its planning by the expressed desires of the members it represents, the available facilities, and the policies of the department.

LEADERSHIP

A full-time recreation director devotes full time to the promotion, organization, and supervision of the clubs. He is assisted by a full-time recreation instructor and several part-time leaders who have special abilities in crafts, music, game and party planning, etc. The age of the leader is not significant, although a near contemporary is likely to have a special awareness of the needs of the aging.

The backbone of the entire program is leadership. Leaders must bring to their assignments sympathy, patience, humility, a willingness and capacity to understand the problems of the older person, and the ability to lead and guide.

The same basic group-work philosophy and principles apply to the old as well as to the young. It is necessary that the leader develop a sensitivity to the needs, feelings, and desires of the individuals in his group and discover opportunities for their recognition and fulfillment. It is important that a leader know when and how and to what extent to take the initiative in program suggestions and organization, and when, how, and to what extent to gradually transfer this to the club officers and committees. His professional knowledge and competence is always important in recognizing the sort of activities that will meet the interest span of members, that will obtain the highest degree of participation, that will help develop wholesome attitudes, that will fit into the time schedules and facilities available, and that will meet the physical limitations of the members.

To help the leader understand the characteristics of the age group with which he is working, the range of personal individual needs, the resources of the community, and the techniques of group leadership which will make his work easier and more effective, the department provides frequent in-service education opportunities, intensive institutes, and timely films and speakers, always supplemented by the opportunity to consult with the director of the program and department specialists on individual problems.

Sample Programs

PROGRAM PLANNING

Programming is done on two levels, club and city-wide. Leadership is guided constantly by the principle that it is not what is done, but what is happening to the individual that is important. Since leadership creates opportunities for new or renewed experiences in social, creative, intellectual, and civic interests, certain characteristic needs are kept in mind:

The aging need the same opportunities for self-expression as any other age level, and those no longer employed may have greater need because of their lost status as workers. They need to feel wanted and respected.

As children move away, contemporaries pass on and neighborhoods change, the lost affection and interest of old friends and acquaintances must be replaced by new.

As their personal circles narrow, they need the sense of belonging and possessing that grows in the fellowship of the club, the security of a clubroom, the cooperation with the council, and the sponsorship of the community.

As their ability to contribute to the economic life of the community shrinks, opportunities for significant service in other areas of community life must be opened.

All of this may be summed up in the statement that THE AGING, LIKE ALL OTHER PEOPLE, NEED TO FEEL THAT THEY COUNT AS PERSONS.

PROGRAM DEVELOPMENT

It is suggested that all leaders keep a file of program suggestions, lists of speakers, newspaper items that carry ideas, picnic spots, interesting trips and outings, timely poems, articles, etc. A record of former successful programs for further reference is also helpful. These suggestions are often exchanged at council and committee meetings, or at leader training institutes, and make for constant enrichment of the total program.

In the area of club planning, the following suggestions have been found of value:

Birthday Recognition. All birthdays which occur during the month are observed at a monthly party with birthday cake, ice cream, birthday cards, and by singing "Happy Birthday." Candy and table favors have also been heart winners. Those who have birthdays are seated at a special table.

Music. Group singing, especially of "old favorites," is very popular. Members are encouraged to sing solos or duets, and in trios, quartettes or small choruses. Those who play an instrument or do "old time dancing" are encouraged to perform, and often reveal many hidden talents. Many older folks have extraordinary talents and skills that the years have strengthened. All they need is a bit of recognition and an opportunity to perform.

Movies. Travel, colored pictures, some comedy, and now and then an educational film seem to be most popular with club members. Air, bus, train lines, and other commercial and industrial concerns are sources for films.

Armchair Travels. People whose hobby is traveling and who take pleasure in sharing their films and colored slides with others often present "travel talks." An invitation to them to appear before a Golden Age Club is usually accepted with great pleasure.

Cards, Games, Etc. This type of entertainment is very popular with most members. Table and circle games, however, need much encouragement. No matter how old an individual is, he or she can continue to learn through play.

Special Parties. Hallowe'en, Christmas, St. Patrick's Day, St. Valentine's Day, Easter, etc., are observed by special parties. Volunteer committees plan the games, refreshments, and programs with the leaders.

Club Participation by the Individual. Membership participation is often the measure of the strengths of a group. The leader's objective is to create a situation that will draw individual members out of their shells into the life of the group where they will feel wanted and needed. Even the shyest person will be encouraged if he or she has something definite to do, such as:

> Welcoming and greeting regular and new members.
> Preparing and serving refreshments.
> Writing cards and letters.
> Calling on shut-ins.
> Keeping attendance records.
> Washing dishes and cleaning up.
> Recording all money contributions and disbursements.

When the club members find something to do in the group which brings them recognition, they have a tendency to cling to their responsibilities.

Another objective of the leader is to gradually encourage the group to develop a high degree of self-direction. In almost every group there are capable, natural leaders. Experts agree that membership can assume and enjoys carrying some of the responsibility of conducting activity. The extent to which this is true naturally varies widely from group to group.

Community Participation by the Individual. The person who lives for himself alone is only partly living. At all ages, the need to be useful, to be of service to others, must be met if an individual is to achieve the fullest satisfactions in life. It is especially important to find ways in which the older person, who considers himself no longer important or of use to anyone, can meet this need.

While the Golden Agers are busy with their own interests and activities, they too want to contribute their share to the community. Throughout the year, they take an active part in the Friendly Visitors Program, Community Chest, the Good Will Industries' Open House, Anti-Tuberculosis Association (filing X-Ray charts), Easter Seal Society (stuffing envelopes for mailing), and assisting the Red Cross. In addition, they provide Christmas joy to children and shut-ins, and Christmas concerts are traditional events. These and other opportune services give the members the feeling of doing for others and is evidence of a willingness to help.

ALL-CITY ACTIVITIES

To further extend the opportunities of the senior citizen for revitalizing experiences, many all-city activities are organized by the department and offered with and through the cooperation of the All-City Council. These have resulted in widening circles of friendship and broadening interest horizons, and they grow increasingly popular each year. Some of the programs and projects that have proved outstandingly successful are the following:

Golden Age Club News. A mimeographed club bulletin, prepared by the recreation department from contributions submitted by the clubs, is distributed to the entire membership every other month without charge. It contains news items about the different clubs, individual members, original songs and poems, human interest stories, and letters.

Craft and Hobby Shops. Recognizing that craft and other hobby interests play a significant role in keeping people alert and interested, the recreation department should provide hobby workshops in different parts of the city which senior citizens attend at will. In addition to the pleasure of making things, members take pride in displaying their finished articles at community exhibits and hobby shows.

Hobby Shows. Articles of crocheting, embroidery, knitting, sewing, weaving, woodworking, leathercraft, dolls, collections, and antiques are featured. Ages of entrants range anywhere from sixty to ninety-three years. A center area is devoted to "live demonstrations" where hobbyists are seen in action at their work. Persons can view the display and watch the entertainment offered by the club members.

The daily newspapers and several weeklies cooperate by featuring the event; two of the larger department stores assist by providing window display room for exhibits a full week prior to the show. Participation certificates are awarded to all individuals who take part in one way or another, eliminating the element of competition.

Recognition Week. Because of the interest and deep concern for older people and the need for recognition, a week in May has been set aside to honor our senior citizens. Special programs are held in the various clubs honoring their octogenarians (those members eighty years of age and older). Charters are presented to those groups in existence for five years. These charters carry a founder's date, the name of the club, the date of presentation, and the signature of the head of the department. Members are elated with their charters and display them in a prominent spot at every club meeting.

Lectures and Courses. Lectures sponsored by the department to meet expressed interests have been popular. The first in the series, "Design for Living in the Golden Years," was especially successful. Other courses offered:

The Senior Citizen Takes Stock
Don't be Afraid to Grow Old
Food and Nutrition

Security in the Later Years
Fitness After Sixty
Three-Generation Family
Forum on Aging

Speakers have included nutritionists, doctors, psychiatrists, and specialists. Panel discussions have been an especially successful form of presentation because they encourage audience participation.

Card Tournaments. Sheepshead, Canasta, Five Hundred, and Rummy tournaments are conducted annually. Winners in each division, men and women, are presented with a Certificate of Award.

Bus trips. "Highways are Happy Ways" becomes true also for the Golden Agers as the summer and fall seasons of each year find hundreds of them taking to the roads on specially planned bus trips sponsored by the recreation department.

Great care is exercised in the selection of sight-seeing routes and destinations. Many of the members have had little or no opportunity to do this on their own, and it is a great joy to visit such widely different wonder spots and to eat at the carefully chosen dining spots. Consideration, too, is given to keeping the expense of the trip a very modest sum, as members must pay their own expenses. For the Golden Agers each trip is a wonderful opportunity to travel, to enjoy the special camaraderie of fellow travelers, to explore new country, gain new friends, dine in pleasant and attractive atmospheres, browse around in quaint little gift shops, and sing to their heart's content while the bus wheels are a'rolling. Often, too, the individual's sense of self-reliance is fortified through the experience of being on one's own in a new environment. Trip days are always looked forward to with keen anticipation, and reflected upon happily.

All-City Chorus. The All-City Chorus, composed of

members from the various Golden Age Clubs, meets regularly once a week, both for the joy of singing together and to prepare numbers for presentation from time to time. Some have sung and always will sing; others have just discovered this interest. Each year, the happy climax of the chorus' efforts is the "Gay Nineties Show," which knits into the production variety and stunt acts by other members as well. This production draws capacity houses of fellow members, relatives, and friends.

Picnic. The annual picnic is a get-together for all clubs and has grown increasingly popular. A well-planned program of games draws a good percentage of participation, bearing out the fact that oldsters can and still want to play. Those unable to play form the spectators, while others enjoy a game of cards, other table games, or a period of relaxation. The "coffee hour" brings out picnic baskets and box lunches, and a "sharing" atmosphere prevails. Music is usually supplied, and shuttle service to transport the handicapped and shut-ins is graciously provided by the American Red Cross.

Camp. Through the cooperation of the United Community Service, the Salvation Army, and the department of recreation, a number of Golden Agers have been able to spend a happy, restful week at the Salvation Army Camp. Since the first adventurous souls came back with enthusiastic reports of their experiences, it has become a prized opportunity. The ages of those who attend range from sixty to ninety-one years; oftentimes couples are able to go together. The experience has been a uniquely valuable addition to the program. All the things one can do at a well-planned camp are available—fishing, boating, swimming, horseshoes and other games, and comfortable benches in the shade for conversation and fancy work. Talent shows in the evening and singing in the starlight add the crowning touch to happy days.

Dances. From the middle of January to Easter, regularly

scheduled open Saturday night dances are held in the gymnasium of a centrally located social center. Each time the hall is gaily decorated to correspond with the coming holiday or some general theme. Individual pin-on badges of an appropriate shape or design are given each person as he enters. These are numbered and serve as an attendance count and in the issuing of attendance prizes. Light refreshments may be purchased at the Snack Bar.

The final dance is the annual costume ball. This is a gala event. Most of the costumes are made by the oldsters themselves and present an amazing sight, thrilling to the observer.

"Perfect Attendance" ribbons are awarded to those who were present at every dance of the series.

A King and Queen with Court of Honor are selected each evening.

This form of recreation has become increasingly popular and is an excellent medium for creating a social outlet and weekend entertainment for hundreds.

TV Performances. Of recent origin is the show *The Golden Years,* which appears weekly. It is a television series for people close to, or in, their retiring years. Golden Agers have proven invaluable in demonstrating their talents and relating their experiences in the "Do You Remember" portion of the program. Likewise, it has given the older people a chance to show the community that they are and still want to be considered useful and needed.

Concerts. Another attraction made available to Golden Agers has been the series of concerts entitled "Music Under the Stars," held during July and August. Special season tickets of reserved seats at a greatly reduced rate have brought many members to recognize and enjoy good, entertaining music.

Theater Parties. Several of the downtown theaters have been promoting special matinee performances of such outstanding productions as *Windjammer, Ben Hur,* and the

Cineramas. Here again, members are given the opportunity of seeing beautiful and educational movies for a nominal fee.

On occasion, bus trips are made to nearby cities to take in stage presentations such as *The Music Man, My Fair Lady,* etc., also at a special "block" price.

Some theaters have combined in sponsoring a Golden Age Movie Club, permitting men and women sixty years of age and over to obtain, free of charge, a year's membership card that entitles them to see, at any time, the featured attraction appearing at either show house by merely presenting the card and paying a fifty-cent fee.

Musical Shows. The varied dramatic and musical offerings of opera companies sponsored by the department of recreation offer excellent opportunities for theater parties. Gift tickets for the especially enjoyable musicals often serve as an introduction to this form of entertainment and are much appreciated.

Baseball. Gift tickets to various games often come to the director of the Golden Age Program for member use. After the introductory experience, members are keenly enough interested to want to provide their own follow-up opportunities. Members are picked up by chartered bus at one of the social centers and returned after the event.

PROGRAM STANDARDS

Children's Afternoon Centers

METHOD OF COUNTING ATTENDANCE

The afternoon centers for children are operated two, three, or four afternoons per week from 3:30 P.M. to 5:30 P.M.

At 4:30 P.M., a bell is rung and each class and activity leader counts the number present in his or her room at that time. This attendance figure is recorded on the front of the leader's attendance card. The total of all activity and class attendance figures determines the center attendance for that afternoon. This is called *the building count*.

Throughout the entire afternoon session of two hours, each activity leader keeps a record of the total number of individuals participating in his or her activity. This figure is recorded on the back of the attendance card. This is called *the activity count*.

At the close of the afternoon session, all attendance cards are turned in to the director's office, from which a weekly report is prepared and filed with the central office. Both attendance counts have a definite purpose—one (the building count) determines the popularity and need for the center in that particular neighborhood, and the other (the activity count) determines the interest in and desire for a specific activity.

ESTABLISHED STANDARDS

Core Program

Art and Craft Class	Dance Class	Table Games
Clubs (Boys or Girls)	High Organized Games (Gym)	

Supplementary Activities

Baton Twirling Class	Music	Tumbling Class
Cooking Class	Sewing Class	Monthly Special Events
Drama	Story Telling	
Low Organized Games	Table Tennis Class	

Program Standards

Not less than *four* different activities per session.
Not less than *six* different types of activities per week.

Minimum Attendance

	Per Session	Average Per Week
Two-Sessions per Week Centers	100	200
Three-Sessions per Week Centers	110	330
Four-Sessions per Week Centers	120	480
Five-Sessions per Week Centers	125	600

Evening Centers

The evening centers for teen-agers and adults are operated from two to five evenings per week from 7:15 P.M. to 9:30 P.M.

At 8:30 P.M. a bell is rung, and each class and activity leader counts the number present in his room to determine the *building count* and the *activity count*. In other words, the procedure is the same as that explained for the afternoon centers.

The Program

Each season the director of the center and his area supervisor plan the program to be offered; such program must be approved by the supervisor of programs to determine whether the program is well balanced, meets the department's established standards, and can be conducted within the budget allowance for that center.

A center's program consists of two parts—the base or "Core" program of non-membership activities, which is common to all centers, and the supplementary program, which is determined by the expressed interests of the neighborhood. Consequently, no two center programs are identical.

CORE PROGRAM

High Organized Games (Gym)	Social Recreation
	Table Games
Pocket Billiards	Table Tennis

SUPPLEMENTARY ACTIVITIES*

Sport and Game Classes

Boxing	Gun Safety	Weight Lifting

---

* Other activities may be conducted, depending upon interest and sufficient enrollment.

Conditioning	Gym	Wrestling
Contract Bridge	Tumbling	
Golf	Water Safety	
Clubs		
Boys	Adult	Music
Girls	Drama	Outdoor Edu-
Mixed	Hobby	cation
Dance Classes		
Ballroom	Square	Tap
Miscellaneous Classes		
Arts and Crafts	Citizenship	Needlecraft
Cake Decorating	English to	Sewing
	Foreign Born	

Junior High School Party
Friday evening—7:00–10.00 p.m.
Permit Groups

Self-organized groups are granted the use of facilities for meetings. These activities and their attendance are *not* considered in determining whether the center meets the program standards; only department sponsored activities are taken into consideration.

PROGRAM STANDARDS

	No. of different types of activities per week	No. of sessions of activities per week
Two-Sessions per Week Center	7	11
Three-Sessions per Week Center	9	13
Four-Sessions per Week Center	12	24
Five-Sessions per Week Center	14	30

MINIMUM ATTENDANCE

	Per Session	Average Per Week	Per Month
Two-Sessions per Week Center	150	300	1200
Three-Sessions per Week Center	170	510	2040
Four-Sessions per Week Center	190	760	3040
Five-Sessions per Week Center	210	1050	4200

ILL AND HANDICAPPED

Why is it important to develop a recreation program for ill and handicapped?

Those who work with handicapped children in institutions and in their homes are impressed with the fact that many children with physical handicaps have been cut off from the normal experiences of childhood to which *all children* are entitled.

Some of these severely disabled children have had very little or no contact with persons other than members of their own families.

A great number of these children have had only "spotty" school experience and have had very little opportunity to play with other children. As a result of this lack of experience, many of these children can be considered "socially retarded." If this social deficiency is not corrected by making play opportunities possible for them, many of these children will sustain a psychological disability more serious than their physical one.

It is therefore of vital importance to help these children through recreation to find ways and means of enriching their life experience, to enlarge their opportunities for social growth, and to help them to develop skills that may serve them vocationally at a later date. One of the gravest problems these children face is their attitude towards themselves and the attitude of other persons towards them. A handicapped child needs to gain confidence in his own abilities and needs to have an opportunity to be accepted as an able person by other people. Ideally, it would be desirable to integrate these children with no physical handicaps in the play programs provided for children with no physical handicaps in the public recreation facilities. In some cases, the severity of the disability, plus the lack of social opportunity, has made it necessary to set up specialized programs. We are, therefore, offering a few suggestions as to organization of such programs.

Steps in the Organization

Determine the Need. The first step in organizing a program for handicapped children in your community is to determine the need for such a program. It is necessary to find out how many handicapped children there are in the community and where they are located. This information is not always readily available, but sometimes can be obtained from some or all of the following sources:

1. Visiting nurse service
2. Public school system
3. Schools for the handicapped
4. Health department
5. Social workers in hospitals
6. Community council
7. Societies such as the National Society for Crippled Children and Adults, Inc.—local chapter
8. United Cerebral Palsy Association—local chapter
9. Agencies working with the deaf, blind, mentally retarded, etc.
10. Local pediatricians

Meetings with the Parents of the Children. It is suggested that the second step should be to call a meeting of the parents of the children to obtain the following information:

1. From the parents' point of view what are the recreational needs of their children?
2. Will the program be available to all types of handicapped children—i.e., physically handicapped, mentally handicapped, mentally retarded, deaf, blind, etc.—or will it be limited to certain groups initially?
3. Will the program be a center program or will it possibly develop into a day camp type of program?
4. Will there be separate facilities for the handicapped

children or will they use the same regular facilities?
5. What time of day will the program take place?
   a. During school hours?
   b. After school hours?
   c. On Saturdays?

Need for Community Cooperation in Planning a Program for Handicapped Children in the Public Facility. Oftentimes it is necessary to call upon individuals or service groups within the community for help. Some of the chief problems are:

Transportation. The following are some suggestions as to how transportation may be obtained:

1. By the parents in car pools
2. By the local Red Cross Chapter transportation unit
3. By service clubs, such as the Rotarians, Kiwanis, Shriners, etc.
4. By school bus
5. By volunteer taxi drivers
6. By the Police Department

In any case, if the transportation is done other than by the parents, the driver must be a licensed chauffeur and liability insurance should be carefully looked into.

Local radio stations, television stations and newspapers can also be helpful in publicizing the need for volunteers, equipment, etc.

Assessment of Area and Facilities. In planning a program for handicapped children consideration should be given to proper area and facilities both for fair and inclement weather.

Some type of shelter is a necessity for handicapped children. It would be desirable to have a shelter with a recreation area within it large enough to accommodate all of the children, including those in wheelchairs in inclement weather. The shelter should have ramps and doorways large enough to give ample clearance for wheelchairs. This shelter should include the following:

1. A telephone
2. Adequate drinking water
3. Toilet space
4. First-aid station
5. Place to rest
6. Storage space for recreational materials, clothing of children and staff, wheelchairs, etc.

It would be desirable if this shelter were to include:

1. Cooking facilities
2. A stage
3. A craft shop
4. A fireplace in the recreational area

These latter items, however, are not necessities.

Handicapped children enjoy some of the following types of activities:

ADAPTED SPORTS

1. Clock golf
2. Basketball
3. Volley ball
4. Baseball
5. Shuffleboard
6. Horse shoes
7. Archery
8. Table tennis

CRAFTS

Almost all the crafts can be done by handicapped children and equipment such as the following would be good to have available:

1. Tools
2. Wood
3. Clay
4. Crayons

5. Scissors
6. Paper
7. Scraps of material
8. Yarn
9. Old junk jewelry
10. Knitting needles
11. Crochet hooks
12. Materials for rug-making

Sometimes equipment such as sewing machines, printing equipment, etc., can be donated if asked for through service groups or individuals.

DRAMATIC PLAY

Handicapped children enjoy activities such as:
1. Story acting
2. Puppetry
3. Doll Play

Equipment such as the following would be good to have available:
1. Costume box with costumes
2. Old clothes to dress up in
3. Materials for making puppets
4. Puppet stage
5. A raised platform
6. Lighting equipment
7. Play house
8. Fire engines
9. Gas station
10. Tricycles
11. Wagons
12. Blocks
13. Tin cans and equipment for making a play store, postoffice, doll's corner, etc.

MUSIC

All children enjoy singing and learning to play simple instruments. It would be desirable to have rhythm band instruments plus the following:
1. Ukelele
2. Harmonicas
3. Flageolets
4. Guitar
5. Auto Harp
6. Piano
7. Record player
8. Tape recorder

PICNICS AND PARTIES

All children love picnics and parties and the following items would be good to have available:
1. Portable barbecue
2. Ring burner
3. Pots and pans
4. Picnic tables

There are many cooked foods on the markets that are easy for handicapped children to make:
1. Kool Aid
2. Candy
3. Cookies, etc.

Assessment of Staff. The experience of a number of agencies working with handicapped children seems to indicate that it is important to have well-trained professional staff plus volunteers to properly service the children. It has been suggested that the ratio of staff to children should be no less than 1 to 5.* The ratio depends some-

---

* This ratio refers to professional staff plus volunteers.

what on the severity of the disabilities of the children.

The Staff

IN-SERVICE TRAINING OF STAFF

Although most professional staff in a public recreation facility are familiar with children and with recreation, they may need to have some help concerning children with physical handicaps. This is often best accomplished by holding some in-service training sessions.

In order to arouse the enthusiasm of the professional staff it may be well to start training sessions with some of the films that are now available on the recreational activities of handicapped children. The National Society for Crippled Children and Adults, the International Society for the Welfare of Cripples, and the film libraries of universities all have a number of films showing camp programs with handicapped children. Some organizations, such as the United Cerebral Palsy Association, the Diabetic Association, the National Foundation, also have films which may be helpful in increasing the knowledge of recreation staff in regard to the rehabilitation of handicapped persons.

It is wise to plan to have a local pediatrician who is interested in rehabilitation give the recreation staff some orientation to the general types of handicaps and also to include a practical demonstration of how to put on and take off braces, how to manipulate wheelchairs, how to make observations that may be helpful to parents or the doctors, how to observe signs of fatigue, etc. It is also necessary to have someone give the recreation staff specific instructions as to exactly what to do in case of emergency.

One session of in-service training should be devoted to keeping records of the observations that recreation staff make, as they may be of great value to other agencies or to parents or doctors working with the children and may later serve in helping to place the child vocationally.

If trips to various places of interest are considered as

part of the recreation program, the staff should receive some instruction on proper ways of loading and unloading the children according to the type of transportation used and should be aware of the insurance problems, etc, involved in transporting the children.

The staff may need some information about and a demonstration of how to adapt various recreational activities to meet the needs of the children.

One of the most important aspects of in-service training is to help the staff to understand that the children should be treated in the same way as children with no physical handicaps and should be encouraged to help themselves insofar as they are able. The children should be held to the rules of the game or the social situation, just as children with no physical handicaps. This is most important in relation to the ultimate adjustment of these children to society.

IN-SERVICE TRAINING OF VOLUNTEER STAFF

Volunteers can be useful in many ways in a recreation program in a public facility. They have been used in some programs as follows:

1. To transport children
2. To help children dress, undress, go to the bathroom, etc.
3. To make and serve a mid-morning snack
4. To aid in the recreation program itself
5. To obtain equipment from interested individuals and organizations
6. To facilitate the program in other ways; e.g., keep records, man the telephone, etc.

Volunteers will work very closely with professional staff and so it is advisable, if possible, to include them in the in-service training of the staff itself. If this is not possible, and if the volunteers are working in the program, special in-service training which should include the following

should be given them:
1. Knowledge of children's recreation
2. A knowledge of how to operate wheelchairs
3. Put on and take off braces, etc.
4. A knowledge of recreational activities and any other information that they know should be given them

Emphasis should be placed on the fact that the child with a physical handicap needs to become as self-sufficient as possible. He needs to develop social skills and abilities. It is important for all staff to understand that the child should only be given direct help when needed and should be encouraged to help himself insofar as possible.

Medical Permission. It is important for the recreation staff to have written medical permission from the parents and the individual physicians to participate in the recreation program. It is also important that the physician indicate on this written record any limitations as to activity that the child might have physically.

COMMUNITY MOVIE PROGRAM

Purpose

Certain thoughtfully-written feature films can play a significant role in leading persons of all ages through progressive steps toward new and richer experiences. In communities throughout the country there is a need for less violent social activities. Full-length 16mm feature films can be easily programmed to provide an activity that is as entertaining as it is culturally enriching.

In recent years movies have been shown on playgrounds and in recreation buildings or school buildings otherwise deserted for the summer. Project supervisors and administrators of municipal funds have experienced the value of good quality entertainment films. Spending funds on arts and crafts satisfies just a limited few, while a like amount spent on movies provide the flexibility necessary to reach hundreds.

I. Types of Programs

Children (including handicapped) want comedies, action, animal stories, science fiction or cartoons.

Teenagers are more difficult to reach, but respond enthusiastically to "in" movies that speak in contemporary language.

The Senior Citizen program is the area where the most meaningful strides will be made. In this category the importance is placed on older stars and pleasant memories. A family Film Night can be equally as rewarding. To assure a consistently good turnout make sure all films fill everyone's appetite, avoiding movies that are too juvenile, saccharine, or adult.

II. Facilities Needed

Recreation Center
School Auditorium
City Hall Meeting Room
Church Multi-purpose Room

III. Equipment

One 16mm sound projector (two are ideal for continuous showings), one sturdy table—40" high, a heavy duty extension cord and ground plug adaptor, extra projection lamps and sound bulbs and one 1600' take up reel.

One adequate screen (the size is determined by the distance of projection). Where no screen is available, improvise with a bedsheet or a white or pastel wall. Two speakers, too, for better acoustics and more enjoyment.

All this is available through a school, church, or a local audio-visual dealer.

IV. Personnel

Projectionist/clean-up man
Ticket Taker
Ushers
Note: Children are usually eager to clean up or be ushers for a free pass.

V. Ordering Films

The movie committee decides the number of films to be used and number of showings, specific titles to be ordered and the day of the week and showing time.

IMPORTANT: Send this information to the film distributor at the same time you order your films. Do all your ordering at one time, it will save you time.

Phone or send in your order well in advance, listing your preferred titles and playdates. Always include a few alternate film choices.

Expect the films to arrive one to two days prior to your showing date. Return it promptly to avoid overtime charges. (Insure all return shipments for $200.00 and obtain a Postal receipt. This is inexpensive and protects against loss.)

VI. Offsetting the Cost

From your Activity Budget
Admission charge/freewill donation.
From soft drink, candy, and popcorn sales.
Subsidy from local businessmen.

VII. Publicizing Your Program

To keep the goodwill of the local theater management,

limit your publicity to handbills and posters within your buildings, word of mouth, and in your yearly Park Calendar.

Experience has shown that total success (a well-satisfied audience) depends on advance planning for the little points that are often overlooked. Have your supervisor set-up and check all equipment well in advance of showtime. This includes chairs and bleachers too (most youngsters will enjoy sitting on the floor). Especially for children's showings, post a large sign in front of your building, indicating the time the movie will be over. This is helpful to the mothers so they will know when to return. Your ticket booth should be open approximately 20 minutes prior to showtime. To keep your audience from becoming restless, show a cartoon or short subject during the file-in and seating time. Handicapped children should be seated near the exits so they may leave with a minimum fuss. Using one projector, expect the average reel change to take 3 to 5 minutes. Finally, never miss a chance to plug the next week's movie or tell them to bring a friend.

7

MAINTENANCE

CUSTODIAL WORK PERFORMANCE STANDARDS

Custodial services are primarily of a repetitive nature with the same work being accomplished daily or on a cycle that repeats at uniform intervals. The descriptions given to the tasks to be performed are general and the method used to accomplish the task may affect the time standard. As a regular assignment, one run can provide janitorial services for an area of 12,000 square feet. The time standards listed are based on work sampling studies and generally used by large institutional agencies, state and federal governments. The L.A.F. (local adjustment factor) should be used if unusual circumstances in a maintenance operation exist.

DAILY SUGGESTED CLEAN-UP PROCEDURES

Your recreation center and surrounding grounds must be neat and clean. Proper maintenance procedures ap-

When a recreation center and other buildings are built in the same park, similar design and construction simplify maintenance procedures.

plied at the right time will save the closing of facilities due to repair time. Also, money spent on repairs many times comes from the program budget. Initiate proper maintenance procedures and keep high cleanliness standards, if you wish to avoid repair problems.

Front Entrances and Lobbies

Porches. Pick up door mats and sweep daily. (Pick up dirt and place in containers.)

In emergency situations, we may be compelled to remove snow from porch and steps to safeguard the public.

Door Mats. Pick up mats before cleaning floor. (Mats should be used only when weather conditions demand it.)

Floors. Empty trash containers. Sweep and mop daily or more often as necessary.

Doors and Glass. Remove markings and keep glass and brass clean and polished daily.

Water Fountains. Must be kept sanitarily clean at all times.

Display Cases. Locate in safe place away from direct traffic lanes. Clean glass daily.

Bulletin Boards. Keep orderly. Remove past dated material.

Supervisor's Office

1. Sweep (Move furniture and empty waste baskets.)
2. Remove accumulation from tops of cabinets, files, and desks
3. Dust
4. Mop
5. Replace furniture

Task	Unit	Standard	L.A.F.	Local standard
Floors—Unobstructed areas (such as corridors, unfurnished rooms or halls, etc.)				
Sweep	1,000 sq ft	0.123		
Dust mop	1,000 sq ft	0.086		
Vacuum	1,000 sq ft	0.266		
Damp mop, lightly soiled area	1,000 sq ft	0.267		
Damp mop, heavily soiled area	1,000 sq ft	0.441		
Wet mop, lightly soiled area	1,000 sq ft	0.467		
Wet mop, heavily soiled area	1,000 sq ft	0.611		
Buff with disc type floor machine	1,000 sq ft	0.205		
Strip and rewax	1,000 sq ft	1.022		
Vacuum and buff (cylindrical machine)	1,000 sq ft	0.250		
Floors—Slightly obstructed (such as clerical or professional offices, etc.)				
Sweep	1,000 sq ft	0.195		
Dust mop	1,000 sq ft	0.164		
Vacuum	1,000 sq ft	0.433		
Damp mop, lightly soiled area	1,000 sq ft	0.390		
Damp mop, heavily soiled area	1,000 sq ft	0.511		
Wet mop, lightly soiled area	1,000 sq ft	0.660		
Wet mop, heavily soiled area	1,000 sq ft	0.781		
Buff with disc type floor machine	1,000 sq ft	0.254		
Strip and rewax	1,000 sq ft	1.132		
Vacuum and buff (cylindrical machine)	1,000 sq ft	0.416		
Floors—Obstructed (such as class or training rooms, etc.)				
Sweep	1,000 sq ft	0.231		

Task	Unit	Standard	L.A.F.	Local standard
Dust mop	1,000 sq ft	0.206		
Vacuum	1,000 sq ft	0.533		
Damp mop	1,000 sq ft	0.484		
Wet mop	1,000 sq ft	0.754		
(*NOTE: Heavy traffic is not normal in obstructed areas; apply appropriate times for heavily traveled aisles from applicable areas.*)				
Buff with disc type floor machine	1,000 sq ft	0.303		
Strip and rewax	1,000 sq ft	1.276		
Stairways and Landings				
Sweep stairway (average 13 steps)	each	0.028		
Damp mop stairway (average 13 steps)	each	0.059		
Wet mop stairway (average 13 steps)	each	0.116		
Sweep landing (approx 100 sq ft)	each	0.021		
Damp mop landing (approx 100 sq ft)	each	0.033		
Wet mop landing (approx 100 sq ft)	each	0.052		
Cleaning Toilet and Fixtures				
Water Closets	each	0.035		
Urinals, floor type	each	0.032		
Urinals, wall type	each	0.025		
Wash Basins, sinks	each	0.024		
Crew type wash basins, 5' dia	each	0.015		
Crew type wash basins, ½ circle, 5' dia	each	0.037		
Soap dispensers, clean and fill	each	0.015		
Drinking fountain	each	0.020		

Glass Cleaning

Wash glass partitions, no ladder	100 sq ft	0.238
Wash glass partitions, use ladder	100 sq ft	0.258
Wash mirrors	10 sq ft	0.016
Wash mirrors, 18″ x 48″	each	0.010

Glass Cleaning—Continued

Wash windows, 4 panes over 4, no ladder	100 sq ft	0.258
Wash windows, 4 panes over 4, use ladder	100 sq ft	0.323
Wash windows, 1 pane over 1 or 2 over 2, no ladder	100 sq ft	0.238
Wash windows, 1 pane over 1 or 2 over 2, use ladder	100 sq ft	0.258

Washrooms

Mens, service only	100 sq ft	0.048
Womens, service only	100 sq ft	0.098
(Servicing includes checking and replacing towels, soap, tissues, sanitary napkin dispensers, and pickup loose trash).		
Mens, clean complete	100 sq ft	0.183
Womens, clean complete	100 sq ft	0.248
(Includes cleaning all fixtures, toilets, accessories, refilling expendables, emptying all refuse, floor sweeping and mopping).		

Dusting Furniture and Equipment

Book case, 3 section with glass doors, 13″ x 33″ x 54″	each	0.003
Bulletin board	each	0.004
Cabinet, 2 drawer card file 7″ x 16″ x 18½″	each	0.002

Task	Unit	Standard	L.A.F.	Local standard
Cabinet, storage, 18″ x 36″ x 78″	each	0.018		
Arm chair, upholstered, leather covered ...	each	0.006		
Chair, rotary or typists'	each	0.004		
Clothestree	each	0.005		
Convector, 4″ x 20″ x 56″	each	0.007		
Desks	each	0.019		
Divan, 6′, leather covered	each	0.013		
File, 4 drawer, 18″ x 28″ x 52″	each	0.003		
Lamp, desk, fluorescent, dust and damp wipe tubes .	each	0.007		
Lamp, desk, incandescent	each	0.001		
Locker, 18″ x 21″ x 6′6″	each	0.014		
Partitions, with glass, dust vertical surface, per square feet	100 sq ft	0.031		
Partitions, walls, etc., solid	100 sq ft	0.040		
Picture, frame, dust and damp wipe glass ...	each	0.006		
Rack, clothes, 20″ x 4′ x 3″ x 6′6″	each	0.013		
Radiator, 10″ x 2′ x 6″ x 4′, sides, ends, interior ...	each	0.022		
Stand, smoking, 9″ base 24″ high	each	0.003		
Stand, typewriter, drop leaves	each	0.003		
Table, 30½″ x 34″ x 45″	each	0.006		
Table, conference, 2′ 6½″ x 4′ x 12′ ...	each	0.023		
Fan	each	0.007		
Venetian, blind, 41½″ x 60″, in place	each	0.062		
Desk items, miscellaneous (telephone, ash trays, etc.)	per 3 misc. items.	0.002		

Window ledge	10 lin ft	0.001
Light Fixtures, Clean		
Disassemble, clean and reassemble industrial 2/40 watt fluorescent.	each	0.078
Disassemble, clean and reassemble finned louver 2/40 watt fluorescent.	each	0.137
Disassemble, clean and reassemble finned louver 4/40 watt fluorescent.	each	0.166
Disassemble, clean and reassemble egg crate louver 4/40 watt fluorescent.	each	0.188
Disassemble, clean and reassemble RLM open, removable shade to 300 watt.	each	0.031
Floor and Floor Covering Material—Continued		
Install hardwood strip flooring (1" x 2"–¼") on wood subfloor, including felt.	100 SF	3.32
Install soft wood strip flooring on wood subfloor including felt; power saw:		
Up to 300 SF	100 SF	2.29
301 SF and up	100 SF	1.91
Install 9" x 9" hardwood block flooring on wood and subfloor, including felt:		
Up to 200 SF	10 SF	0.41
201 SF and up	100 SF	3.70
Install 9" x 9" hardwood block flooring on concrete, using sealer and mastic.	100 SF	1.80
Remove old and replace with new single 9" x 9"	each	0.056+

Task	Unit	Standard L.A.F.	Local standard
hardwood flooring blocks at separate locations (N = No. blocks).		N (0.10)	
Remove old and replace with new hardwood flooring blocks at one location (N = No. blocks).	each	0.04+ N (0.074)	
Remove old and replace with new wooden blocks using pitch filter, industrial flooring:			
Up to 10 SF	ea SF	0.12	
11 SF and up	ea SF	0.06	
Remove old and replace with new asphalt tiles individually or in groups, per tile (up to 30 tiles) (N = No. tiles).	each	0.035+ N (0.065)	
Install linoleum on wood floor, including felt underlay	100 SF	1.20	
Install border moulding	10 LF	0.09	
Remove non-glued linoleum on wood floor and install glued linoleum, no underlay.	100 SF	0.64	
Remove old and replace with new glued linoleum on concrete floor, including felt underlay.	100 SF	2.36	
Install asphalt tile on wood floor, includes felt underlay	100 SF	1.78	
Replace asphalt tile on wood floor, includes felt underlay	100 SF	2.98	
Light Fixtures, Clean—Continued			
Disassemble, clean and reassemble RLM open, in place to 300 watt.	each	0.044	

Item	Unit	Value
Disassemble, clean and reassemble vapor or explosion proof with shade to 300 watt.	each	0.091
Disassemble, clean and reassemble vapor or explosion proof without shade to 300 watt.	each	0.027
Disassemble, clean and reassemble recessed 4/40 watt fluorescent.	each	0.132
Disassemble, clean and reassemble open glass globe to 300 watt.	each	0.032
Disassemble, clean and reassemble strip light 1/40 watt fluorescent.	each	0.167
Disassemble, clean and reassemble combination mercury vapor and incandescent.	each	0.092
NOTE: For use of ladder with each operation add	each	0.020
Miscellaneous Cleaning		
Venetian blinds, wash-rinse	each	0.333
Sand urns, clean	each	0.002
GI can, empty	each	0.005
Waste basket, empty (per basket)	10	0.015
Cardboard barrel, empty	each	0.005
Tilt top trash container, empty	each	0.008
Trash container bag, empty	each	0.008
Wash door (both sides and frame)	each	0.139
Wash tile, no ladder	100 sq ft	0.207
Wash tile, use ladder	100 sq ft	0.227

Task	Unit	Standard L.A.F.	Local standard
Wash walls, partitions, no ladder	100 sq ft	0.347	
Wash walls, partitions, use ladder	100 sq ft	0.367	
Wash ceilings, use scaffold or ladder	100 sq ft	0.417	
Wash baseboards or sills, no ladder	100 lin ft	0.497	

Analysis of Custodial Personnel Requirements

Often a recreation center director is required to estimate the maintenance needed for a new recreation center or evaluate the maintenance operations of an existing recreation center. By using a combination of information about the recreation center and maintenance tasks, a recreation center director can achieve a reasonable estimate of the maintenance required.

The following table provides an easy method of calculating the required maintenance. Man hour requirements standards are taken from the preceding table. Daily, weekly, monthly or yearly frequency of maintenance tasks must be determined by the center director based on use of the facility.

Toilet Rooms

1. Remove loose material from floor, sweep and empty trash containers
2. Clean wash basins
3. Wash urinals and flush boxes
4. Wash seats and bowls (Inside and outside.)
5. Remove wall and partition markings
6. Clean metal fittings
7. Check paper holders and ventilate room
8. Mop floor

Shower Rooms

1. Remove soap stains from walls and floor; also clear floor drains
2. Scrub walls and floor with soap solution (Use bank deck brush.)
3. Hose down and thoroughly rinse

ANALYSIS OF CUSTODIAL PERSONNEL REQUIREMENTS														☒ MONTHLY ☐ ANNUALLY
				FLOOR CLEANING										
BUILDING NO. AND USE	SPACE SERVICED	TYPE OF FLOOR SURFACE	AREA (Sq. Ft.)	SWEEP		DUST MOP		DAMP MOP		VACUUMING		BUFFING		STR REW
				F	M-H	F	M-H	F	M-H	F	M-H	M	M-H	F
1 REC. CENTER 1/2 BASMT		ASPH. T.	5,000	D	22			W	16			W	13	M2
2 #1	1ST FL.	VINYL T.	10,000	D	41			W	31			W	25	M1
3														
4 REC. CENTER 1ST FL.		VINYL T.	14,100			D	95					M	8	M
5 #2	2ND FL.	VINYL T.	5,700			D	18	W	16			W	13	M2
6														
7 ELEMENTARY 1ST FL.		CONC.	11,000	D	48			M	9					
8 SCHOOL 2ND FL.		ASPH. T.	9,600			D	52	W	32			W	29	M2
9														
10														
11														
12														
13														
14														
15														
16														
17														
18														
19														
20				NOTE: THE BUILDINGS IN THIS SAMPLE ANALYSIS										
21				WERE CHOSEN TO ILLUSTRATE A WIDE RANGE										
22				OF JANITORIAL OPERATIONS. MOST OTHER										
23				TYPES OF BUILDINGS FOR WHICH										
24				JANITORIAL SERVICE PROVIDED WILL										
25				REQUIRE FEWER MANHOURS.										
26														
27														
28														
29														
30														
31														
32			59,800 sq. ft.											
33		TOTAL			111		115		109				23	

D— DAILY	2M— TWICE MONTHLY	MS— EVERY 6 MONTHS
W— WEEKLY	M2— EVERY 2 MONTHS	Y— YEARLY
2W— TWICE WEEKLY	M3— EVERY 3 MONTHS	O— OTHER (Specify)
M— MONTHLY	M4— EVERY 4 MONTHS	

TOILET AND FIXTURE CLEANING

CYLINDRICAL MACHINE		DRY CLEAN WAXING BUFFING		WATER CLOSETS		URINALS		SINKS/ WASHBOWLS		DRINKING FOUNTAINS		FLOORS		WALLS PARTITIONS WOODWORK		DISPENSER (Filling or cleaning)	
		F	M—H	NO/F	M—H	NO/F	M—H	NO/F	M—H	NO/F	M H	SF/F	M H	SF/F	M H	NO/F	M H
				3/D	2½	1/D	1	2/D	2	1/D	1	150/D	4½	115/M	2½	7/D	2
				5/D	6½	2/D	2	3/D	3½	1/D	1	24/D	7	1000/M	3½	9/D	2½
		Touch up W 8		9/D	16	4/D	9½	5/D	5½	3/D	2	534/D	13	142/M	6½	19/D	5
				7/D	7½	4/D	9½	6/D	6½	1/D	1	356/D	9	12·16/M	5	21/D	6
				6/D	6½	9/D	9½	6/D	6½	1/D	1	77/D	7	840/M	3½	15/D	7

COMPUTATION OF PERSONNEL REQUIRED

ITEM 1 — PRODUCTIVE MANHOURS .... 929 ¼

ITEM 2 — 20% OF ITEM NO 1 .... 185 ¾

ITEM 3 — TOTAL HOURS 1115

ITEM 4 — PERSONNEL REQUIRED .... 1115 (TOTAL HOURS) = 6.9 OR 6
                                        174 (HOURS PER MONTH)

| | 8 | | | 33 | | 16½ | | 29 | | 6 | | 40½ | | 26 | | 11½ | |

MAN-HOUR AND PERSONNEL REQUIREMENTS																
1. PRODUCTIVE MAN-HOURS 921 1/4	2. PAID UNPRODUCTION TIME (20% of Item 1 for travel between bldg, field supervision, leave and holidays) 1/5 3/4								3. TOTAL HOURS (Item 1 plus Item 2) 1115							
	GLASS CLEANING				DUSTING											
	WINDOWS		MIRRORS INTERIOR GLASS		FURNITURE		WALLS CEILINGS PIPES SCREENS		WINDOW BLINDS SHADES		VENETIAN BLINDS		LIGHT FIXTURES		RADIATORS/ UNIT HEATERS	
	NO/F	M H	NO/F	M H	PC/F	M H	F	M H	NO/F	M H	NO/F	M H	NO/F	M H	NO/F	M H
	2/mq	1	2/yr		3/10	9	m-i	1/2	1/m	1/2	4/mq	1 1/2	2/mq	1/2	11/yr	2
	13/mq	9 1/2	3/yr		152/2w	18	mq	1	2c/m	1	2c/md	6	2c/m3	1	21/m	9 1/2
	24/mq	2	4/w		26/10	24	mq	3	3/m	1/2	3/mq	2 1/2	2c2/mq	1 1/2		
	13/mq	1			1/10	9	mq	1	12/m	1/4	2/md	1	2/m3	1		
	2/mq	5	3/w		52/10	7	mq	2 1/2	2/m	1 1/4	2/md	2	13/mq3	1/2	15/m	3
	73/mq	9 1/2	2/w		208/10	24	mq	2	24/m	1 1/4	2c/md	6	14/m3	1	16/m	2 1/2
	HRS) = 6.9 CB 6															
	PER MONTH)															
	180				91		10		4 3/4		14		6 1/2		12	

4 PERSONNEL REQUIRED (Divide total monthly hours, Item 3, by 174, annually by 2088)		AS OF DATE 1 JULY 1970	CENTER

MISCELLANEOUS CLEANING

AIR CONDITIONING GRILLES		RUGS		WALLS PARTITIONS WOODWORK		SPOT CLEAN (Walls or partitions)		FURNITURE (Washing or polishing)		STAIRWAYS		ENTRANCES		SAND URNS ASH TRAYS WASTE BASKETS TRASH REMOVAL		PRODUCTIVE MAN HOURS
NO/F	M H	SF/F	M H	F	M H	F	M H	PC/F	M H	NO/F	M-H	NO/F	M H	F	M H	
				Y	1½			3/M=2	2/D	1	2/D	1	0	7	101
				Y	3			7/M=3½					0	19	200¼
2½/M=1	1			Y	8			113/M=5½	1/D	½	2/D	1	0	15	199
1/M=½	½			Y	3			59/M=3					0	6	78¾
				Y	2			3/M=2	2/D	1	2/D	1	0	9	138¾
				Y	6½			11/M=5½					0	2	211¼
	½				30				21½		2½		3	58	929¼

Locker Rooms

1. Clean inside and tops of lockers (Use damp cloth.)
2. Dressing booths must be sanitarily cleaned
3. Sweep floor
4. Mop
5. Squeegee shere drains are provided

Auditoriums, Stages, Club Rooms and Artcraft Rooms

1. Move furniture
2. Sweep (Empty waste containers.)
3. Remove wall markings
4. Mop or mop and wax
5. Dust thoroughly
6. Replace furniture

Kitchens

1. Clean and wash all top surfaces (Tables, sinks, shelves, stoves, refrigerators, etc.)
2. Dust thoroughly (Ledges, moldings, etc.)
3. Sweep floor (Move furniture where necessary.)
4. Mop

Janitor's Closets

1. Mop sink must be clean at all times
2. Keep shelves neat and orderly
3. Floors to be cleaned as per recommendation
4. Tools must be hung orderly and mops washed before hanging
5. Pails shall be stored upside down

Craft Shops

1. Dust light fixtures, moldings, etc.

2. Sweep floor (Empty waste containers.)
3. Do not disturb items left on work benches or machinery
4. Craft shop classes shall assist in cleaning up their own area of operation at the direction of the craft instructor

Storerooms

1. All material and equipment must be stored orderly and accessibly
2. Inventory of cleaning materials and supplies must be made monthly and the next month's needs noted for the Supervisor's record
3. *Beware of fire hazards*

Gymnasiums

1. Move equipment where possible
2. Pick up loose material
3. Sweep with yarn floor brush
4. Remove gum spots
5. Spray revivor mist over entire area. Allow one half hour for settling (Hard wood floors only.)
6. Remove stubborn rubber burns (individually)
7. Sweep with yarn floor brush

Indoor Pool Decks

1. Hose down and squeegee daily
2. Scrub with neutral* soap solution as needed
3. Hose liberally to properly rinse
4. Squeegee

---

* Neutral Soap: A soap that is neither acid or alkaline, therefore safe to use on any type surface.

CLEANING AGENTS

Cleaning agents commonly used in custodial services may be divided into two general classes: those emulsifying dirt with water, and those removing it by abrasive action. Some cleaning agents combine these actions.

Emulsifying Agents

Soaps. Consist of fats or oils combined with an alkali of sodium or potassium. Strong soaps, such as yellow GI, are made from an alkali of sodium and fat and have an excess of free alkali. Toilet and hand soaps are usually made with palm, coconut, or cottonseed oils and alkalies of sodium or potassium and have a low free alkali content.

Liquid Hand Soap. Is similar to toilet soaps but is in solution with water. The soap content varies from 15 to 42 percent.

SOAP SUBSTITUTES

Detergents. Detergents have largely replaced soaps for the various cleaning processes in custodial services. The standard detergent for these processes is known as "All-Purpose Synthetic Detergent Cleaning Compound," meeting the requirements of Federal Specification No. PC 431. The detergent comes in powder or flakes, liquid, and paste and contains no abrasives or fatty acid soaps and is not irritating to the skin. It is excellent for cleaning painted surfaces, asphalt or rubber tile, and sheet floor coverings.

Trisodium Phosphate. Is an inexpensive, strong cleaning agent. It is especially effective for removing grease and oil. It should not be used for cleaning painted surfaces, except for heavily soiled areas that cannot be cleaned with detergents, and then in only weak solutions. Trisodium-phosphate *should not* be used on wood, linoleum, asphalt or rubber tile, or oxychloride floors.

Scouring Powder

Scouring powder is a combination of soap powder and abrasives, such as powdered quartz, feldspar, marble, lava, or pumice. In order to prevent serious scratching of surfaces, these abrasives should pass through a number 100 sieve. Trisodium phosphate may be added to improve the cleaning properties of the powder. They should not be used on marble, terrazzo, asphalt tile, rubber tile, linoleum, wood floors, painted surfaces, or as metal polish, and should be used with care on ceramic and quarry tile.

IMPORTANT: If cleaning is done regularly and properly, there should be little need for use of scouring powder.

Precautions in Use of Cleaning Agents

Cleaning agents attack surfaces as well as dirt or grime. When cleaning agents are used, there is some damage to surfaces. In order to clean and do as little damage as possible, these rules should be followed:

1. Never use washing solution stronger than necessary. Directions for preparing washing solutions are given in this manual.
2. Apply washing solution only long enough to loosen dirt.
3. Rinse cleaned surfaces with clear water.
4. Do not spill washing solution on surfaces not to be cleaned. Particular care should be taken not to splash cleaning agents against kalsomined or casein-painted walls, because it is impossible to wipe without spotting wall. In other cases, spilled solution should be wiped up immediately with clean cloth.
5. Use steel wool, scouring powders, and abrasives only when absolutely necessary. When used, care should be taken to prevent damage to surface cleaned.

Stain Removers

Stain removers can clean in three ways; by dissolving substance causing stain, by acting as bleaching agent, or by absorbing substance causing stain. Most stains can be removed by methods recommended in the Stain Chart.

In some instances, water causes stains on washbowls, urinals, and toilet bowls. Daily cleaning with all-purpose synthetic detergent solution will remove these stains. If fixtures are badly stained, use soapgrit cake and damp cloth. If this fails, mix a weak solution of sodium bisulfate (toilet bowl cleaner) and apply with cloth attached to a stick. Leave solution on stain long enough to remove it. Wash with allpurpose synthetic detergent solution thoroughly. Repeated use of toilet bowl cleaner will remove glaze from porcelain and porcelain enameled fixtures, making them impossible to clean satisfactorily. Do not use acids such as muriatic, oxalic, or hyperchlorous to remove stains on porcelain. They destroy surface glaze very quickly.

Abrasive Cleaners

Abrasive cleaners contain sharp grit particles which vary in size and hardness. Soap-grit cake and scouring powders also contain these abrasives. Particles should be fine enough to pass through a number 100 sieve. Soap-grit cake should not be used to polish metal. If plumbing fixtures are properly cleaned daily, there should be little need for use of abrasives.

Polishing Agents

Metal Polish. Metal polish is made from fine abrasive and cleaner such as soap or soap powder. Abrasive removes tarnished surface of metal, soap helps carry it away.

Furniture Polish. Furniture polish should remove dirt, leave a gloss or sheen, and protect surfaces. It is applied manually with a dampened cloth pad. Some polishes consist only of light oil which provides gloss as long as surfaces are wet. Others contain waxes mixed with oil which brighten and protect surfaces after oil evaporates. Polish should not leave surfaces oily or sticky, should not injure varnish or enamel, and dust should not stick to it. Good polish may be made by dissolving one-half pound of carnauba wax in one gallon of turpentine at room temperature.

Waxes and Finishes

Waxes may be made of animal, vegetable, mineral, or synthetic origin. Best known vegetable wax is carnauba. It is the hardest and most durable of waxes. Nearly all good wax products contain some carnauba. Waxes are waterproof, and may be dissolved in alcohol, turpentine, or mineral spirits. Good floor wax has a high melting point, is hard, and takes high polish.

Mineral Spirit and Paste Wax. These waxes, because of the fire hazard involved, are to be used only on approval by the custodial supervisor.

WATER EMULSION WAX

General. Water emulsion wax consists of carnauba wax, resin, and emulsifying materials in 12 percent and 16 percent concentrations. Drops of wax are held in suspension. Ammonia is sometimes added to make emulsion more waterproof after drying. After application, water evaporates, leaving wax in tiny drops which have a sheen or gloss. For this reason, water emulsion wax does not need buffing to look well. However, buffing makes wax stick better, wear better, and makes it more waterproof. Specification P-W-155 governs the specifications for water emulsion wax.

Precautions in Handling Water Emulsion Wax. Water emulsion wax is a delicate solution. Adding water, freezing, or using a dirty mop or container breaks down its properties. It is important, therefore to prevent wax from freezing, and to use clean mops and containers.

BAR WAX

General. Bar wax is a mixture of pure carnauba wax and nonslip resins. It is cast in bars and contains no solvents.

Use of Bar Wax. Bar wax is used on cylindrical type dry-cleaning machine. It rides on brush or steel wool drum. One bar will cover between 8000 and 15,000 square feet. Bar wax may be used on all floor surfaces.

Resin Emulsion Floor Finishes. This type floor finish contains no wax and is usually composed, in whole or in part, of acrylic, polyethylene, and polyvinyl resins in emulsion with water. The finishes have not been developed sufficiently to replace water emulsion wax for general use. However, the finishes usually require no buffing and are slip-resistant. For these reasons they are particularly suitable for use where buffers are not available, in congested areas where the use of buffers is difficult, and where slip resistance is important, such as on ramps.

Floor Oil

General. One type of floor oil consists of linseed oil and turpentine or mineral spirits. When applied to floor it penetrates, and dries to a fairly hard, non-oily surface. Another type, a paraffin-base floor oil, penetrates wood, but does not harden. This leaves floor slippery until oil is washed off or worn away. While floor oils serve to control dust, they also present disadvantages. Oils darken wood floors, soil objects dropped, and soften fibers of many woods, reducing wearing quality. When oiled floors are mopped, soap emulsifies oil and quickly removes it.

Use of Floor Oil. Floor oil should be used only when floors are in such condition that they cannot be sealed satisfactorily and dust control is important. Floor oils present a fire hazard, and must be used carefully. Oils must *not* be used where a fire hazard is inherent in the work which is done in the area.

Disinfectants

Disinfectants are designed to kill germs and may consist of phenol (carbolic acid), pine oil, cresol, creosote, or cresylic acid. They kill germs by coming in contact with them and must be applied directly. If floors are kept clean, toilet rooms are at satisfactory standard of cleanliness, and waste is disposed of properly, germs have small chance of breeding. A well-kept building does not require disinfectants.

CAUTION: Disinfectants are poisons.

Deodorants

Deodorants are used to eliminate disagreeable odors. When deodorants are necessary, it is an indication the area is not properly cleaned and ventilated. Deodorants are unpleasant to many people.

STAIN REMOVAL CHART

Stain	On wood	On linoleum	On asphalt tile	On vinyl	On marble, terrazzo, or oxychloride cement	On concrete
Blood	Rub with cloth dampened in clear cold water. If stain persists, dampen cloth with ammonia.	Same as for wood.	Same as for wood.	Same as for wood.	Rub with cloth dampened in clear cold water. Bleach with peroxide, if stain persists.	Same as for marble.
Grease or oil	Pour kerosene on spot. Permit to soak for a short time. Wipe dry with a clean cloth. Wash with all-purpose synthetic detergent solution, rinse dry.	Scrub with warm all-purpose synthetic detergent solution. Rinse with clear water.	Same as for linoleum.	Same as for wood.	Pour solvent on spot, cover with Fuller's earth and let stand for several hours. Repeat, if necessary.	Pour alcohol on spot. Rub on spot. Rub with clean cloth.
Ink	Apply solution 1 part oxalic acid crystals to 9 parts warm water. Permit to	Use warm all-purpose synthetic detergent solution. If stain per-	Same as for linoleum.	Wash with all-purpose synthetic detergent, rinse, then	Same as for linoleum.	Same as for linoleum.

water.			with cloth dampened with ammonia.		Apply alcohol and rub with clean cloth.
Iodine or mercurochrome	perborate in pint of hot water. Mix whiting to form paste. Apply to spot and let dry.	Apply alcohol and rub with clean cloth.	Same as for wood.	Warm neutral soap solution.	Apply alcohol and cover with Fuller's earth.	Apply alcohol and rub with clean cloth.
Paint	Use oxalic acid solution, or 1 lb trisodium phosphate in 1 gal warm water.	Rub with No. 0 steel wool dipped in turpentine. Wash with all-purpose synthetic detergent solution and rinse.	Rub with steel wool and all-purpose synthetic detergent solution. If area is large, use steel wool on buffing machine.	Rub with No. 0 steel wool dipped in all-purpose synthetic solution.	Rub with No. 00 steel wool dipped in turpentine.	Scrub with 1 lb. trisodium phosphate in 1 gal. hot water, rinse with clear water.

(Cont'd)

Rust	Wash with all-purpose synthetic detergent. Rub with No. 0 steel wool, if necessary.	Apply solution 1 part oxalic acid to 9 parts warm water. Let dry. Rinse thoroughly with clear water.	Rub with No. 0 steel wool and synthetic detergent solution.	Same as for linoleum.	*Horizontal Surfaces* To ¾ gal water add 1.9 lb. sodium citrate and 1 lb. sodium hydrosulfite. Add enough water to make a gallon solution. Cover stain with solution and let stand ½ hour. Absorb with cloth by rubbing. Rinse with clear water. *Vertical Surfaces* Make paste with whiting and 3 oz. sodium citrate and 3 oz. sodium hydrosulfite. Apply with putty knife and allow to remain 1 hr. Wash with sodium citrate.	Same as for marble.
Sole and heel	Rub with No. 0 steel wool or wash with all-	Same as for wood.	Same as for wood.	Rub with No. 0 steel wool dipped	Wash with all-purpose synthetic detergent	Same as for marble.

	tic detergent solution.		pose synthetic detergent solution.	rinse.	

Stain	On wood	On linoleum	On asphalt tile	On vinyl	On marble, terrazzo, or oxychloride cement	On concrete
Chewing gum	Remove gum with putty knife. Apply alcohol, rub with clean cloth.	Same as for wood.	Remove gum with putty knife. Do not use alcohol on asphalt tile.	Remove as much as possible with putty knife. Rub with No. 0 steel wool dipped in all-purpose synthetic detergent solution.	Same as for wood.	Same as for wood.

Stain — On wood
Stain — On linoleum
Stain — On asphalt tile
Stain — On vinyl
Stain — On marble, terrazzo, or oxychloride cement
Stain — On concrete

Stain — On wood
Stain — On linoleum
Stain — On asphalt tile
Stain — On vinyl
Stain — On marble, terrazzo, or oxychloride cement
Stain — On concrete

Attractive landscaping for a recreation center should be planned for in the initial design. Proper budgeting for maintenance will insure that the landscaping will receive proper care.

CLEANING METHODS

Floor Cleaning

Floors are cleaned to maintain sanitary working conditions, to make them attractive, and to preserve them from damage. Methods suggested in this manual result from practical experience and research.

SWEEPING

Dirt can be removed by a vacuum cleaner, sweeping

with a brush or broom, or the use of a dry or treated sweeping mop.

Sweeping Tools. Sweeping tools used on various kinds of floor coverings are shown in the following chart. Offices and other areas containing equipment should be swept with medium size brooms or sweeping mops. An 18- to 36-inch broom or sweeping mop should be used for corridors. A V-type sweeping mop that may be adjusted in width from 6 to 57 inches serves both purposes. Neither bristle brushes nor sweeping mops are used to pick up heavy dirt or mud. Corn brooms are used for this purpose. Dirt gathered by brush, broom, or V-type sweeping mop is picked up in a dustpan and emptied into a dustbox. Dirt and dust from straight sweeping mops is shaken directly into the dustbox. Detailed instructions for handling and use of sweeping tools are given in Section A.

Frequency of Sweeping. Frequency of sweeping depends on the nature of the business carried on in the building, amount of floor traffic, and local conditions, such as weather, nature of soil, condition of grass around buildings, and adequacy of sidewalks.

Sweeping Standard. A properly swept floor should not have dust streaks, marks where dirt was picked up with dustpan, dirt in corners, behind radiators or doors, or under furniture. Furniture and other equipment moved during sweeping should be replaced. Baseboards, equipment, and furniture should not be disfigured by sweeping mop or broom. The room should appear orderly and well attended.

MOPPING

General. Mopping removes dirt which sticks to the floor surface and cannot be removed by sweeping, or by dry cleaning. Water and soap loosen and dissolve the dirt so it may be removed. The mop is used to spread washing solution and rinse water, to rub sticky dirt loose from the floor, and to pick up washing solution and rinse water.

Extensive damage has occurred from use of excessive water, and strong cleaning agents. Damage will be avoided by strict adherence to the following rules:

1. Use water sparingly, only enough to do the job.
2. Never use a mopping solution stronger than necessary.
3. Allow water to loosen dirt, then remove.
4. Mop, rinse, and dry one small area of floor at a time. This reduces time water remains on floor.
5. Change both wash and rinse water frequently.
6. Splashing baseboards, furniture or other equipment should be avoided. If legs of furniture become dark from mop water or wax, wash with soft cloth and solution of warm water and all-purpose synthetic detergent solution. Rinse with clear water, and dry with a clean cloth.
7. Water should not be allowed to seep under baseboards, furniture, or other equipment.
8. Difficult places, such as corners or behind radiators, should be mopped by hand.

Frequency of Damp Mopping. Frequency of damp mopping will depend on weather conditions, amount of traffic, and type of floor surface. Rough or porous floors need mopping more often than smooth, sealed floors.

SCRUBBING

Floors should be scrubbed only when they cannot be cleaned satisfactorily by mopping. Scrubbing is performed with a brush which may or may not have a handle. The general rules for mopping apply. If scouring powder must be used, sprinkle powder lightly on floor before scrubbing. When using solutions stronger than all-purpose synthetic detergent solution, wear rubber gloves to protect the hands. Water or scrubbing solution should not remain on floor longer than absolutely necessary. Wood floors should be scrubbed with the grain.

IMPORTANT: Floor scrubbing should be kept to an absolute minimum. If floors are properly maintained, they seldom need scrubbing.

SWEEPING TOOLS USED ON
DIFFERENT KINDS OF FLOORS

Kind of floor surface	Bristle floor brush	Fiber floor brush	Corn broom	Sweeping mop Treated	Sweeping mop Untreated
Rough, unpainted, or unsealed open-grain wood floor		XX	X		
Smooth, unpainted, or unsealed wood floor	X	XX			
Smooth, sealed, or painted wood floor—not waxed	X			XX	
Smooth, sealed, and waxed wood floor	X				XX
Linoleum—waxed					XX
Asphalt tile—not waxed	X				XX
Asphalt tile—waxed	X				XX
Vinyl—not waxed	X			XX	XX
Vinyl—waxed	X				XX
Terrazzo					XX
Mosaic tile				XX	XX
Quarry tile				XX	XX
Rubber tile	X				XX
Rubber tile—waxed	X				XX
Rough concrete		XX	X		
Smooth concrete—not treated to eliminate dustiness	X	XX			
Smooth, treated, or painted concrete	X	X·		XX	XX
Oxychloride cement	X				XX

Note: XX means that the tool is to be used if equipment is available. X means that the tool is to be used only if tool marked XX is not available. Where two tools are checked with the same symbol, either may be used.

MOPPING SOLUTIONS

Kind of floor surface	Mopping solution	Wet mop scrubbing	Damp mop	Rinse	Remarks
Unpainted, unsealed wood	⅛ to 1 cup of synthetic detergent in 1 gal. of water.	Only if very dirty, or dirt has set.	Preferred. Use as little as possible.	Yes. Change water often.	Avoid alkalies; GI soaps or strong solutions of tri-sodium phosphate emulsify oils and gums in wood. Water softens fibers causing rapid wear. Remove water immediately.
Sealed wood or painted wood, not waxed	⅛ to ¼ cup of synthetic detergent in 1 gal. of water.	Only if very dirty, or dirt has set.	Preferred. Use as little water as possible.	Yes. Change water often.	While paint and seals are not attacked by water, they are by alkali GI soap, and all strong cleaning solutions. Rinse carefully and remove water immediately.
Waxed wood, linoleum, asphalt tile, vinyl	Clear water and small amount of synthetic detergent only.	Only to remove wax.	Yes. Use as little water as possible.		Do not use soap or any other cleaning agent except to remove dirt. Mop only if floor cannot be dry cleaned.

Floor type	Cleaning agent	Wet mopping	Damp mopping	Scrubbing	Remarks
Unwaxed linoleum, asphalt tile, rubber, mastipave, vinyl	Clear water. If very dirty, use all-purpose synthetic detergent solution.	Never let water stand on these floors. Water in seams loosens floor coverings.	Yes. Use as little water as possible.		These floor coverings are impervious to most dirt, and clear water will remove everything except grease and some stains. Alkali GI soap emulsifies linseed oil in linoleum. Strong trisodium phosphate is equally destructive.
Unwaxed oxychloride cement	Clear water. If very dirty, use all-purpose synthetic detergent solution.	Only if very dirty. Change solution often.	Preferred. Change water often.	Yes. Change water often.	Strong acids or alkalies attack floors and cause deterioration. Mild acids and alkalies scar them.
Terrazzo, mosaic tile, flagstone, slate, marble, unpainted concrete	All-purpose synthetic detergent solution.	Only if very dirty. Change solution often.	Preferred. Change water often.	Yes. Change water often.	Alkali GI soaps and strong solutions of trisodium phosphate attack marble, slate, terrazzo, and the like and cause pitting and rapid wear.
Painted concrete	Same as for painted wood.	Only if very dirty.	Preferred.	Yes.	See remarks on painted wood floors.

OUTLINES OF JANITORIAL OPERATIONS FOR ON-THE-JOB USE

General

REQUISITION FOR MAINTENANCE OR TRANSFER

All requests for maintenance to be done at facilities under the jurisdiction of the Recreation Commission will be submitted to the supervisor *in duplicate* on a "Request for Maintenance or Transfer" form (shown in Appendix). The request should be made by the Director. If at any time it is necessary to have maintenance done immediately, call the Recreation office at once and complete the maintenance request form as soon as possible.

CARE OF EQUIPMENT

Expendable equipment such as basketballs, softballs, bats, etc., should be:

1. Used only for what it is intended
2. Kept clean
3. Kept repaired
4. Kept in its proper or designated place
5. Taken back to place of purchase if defective and reported to supervisor

Outlines

A. TREATING SWEEPING MOPS, YARN DUSTERS, AND DUSTCLOTHS

Equipment needed:

1. Hand spray gun
2. Metal mop pan 8" wide, 8" high, 24" long with cover
3. Large mop bucket
4. Container for glycol mixture

Materials needed:

1. Hot and cold water
2. Polyethylene glycol compound

Mixing the solutions:

Mix polyethylene glycol with water in ratio of 3 parts water to 1 glycol.

Getting mops ready:

1. Before treatment, new mops, dusters, and cloths require soaking in hot water. Soaking tightens the yarn.
2. Old mops or dusters do not require soaking before treatment, but should be washed clean in solution of 1 tablespoon trisodium phosphate to 1 gallon of warm water, and then rinsed thoroughly.

Doing the job:

1. After mops have dried and yarn is straightened and combed, mop should be placed bottom up and sprayed with glycol solution using about 1½ ounces for 1 pound mops, and 2 ounces for 1¼ pound mops.
2. Properly treated mop will be fluffy and light to handle. It will not feel damp or yarn will not be soggy or matted.
3. After treatment, fold mop yarn together, roll tightly, and place in closed metal container for about eight hours. This allows solution to spread evenly throughout the mop. Treat dusters and cloths similarly.

Care of equipment:

1. Clean all equipment thoroughly
2. Remove spots from floor or table
3. Dispose of wiping cloths
4. Return all supplies and equipment to their proper storage places

B. WASHING SWEEPING MOPS, DUSTERS, AND DUSTCLOTHS

Equipment needed:

1. Mop bucket, large can or bucket and wringer or squeezer

   2. Palmetto brush

   3. Plumber's "friend" (rubber force cup with handle) or broom handle

Materials needed:

   1. Warm water

   2. Trisodium phosphate

Getting mop heads, dusters, or dustcloths ready:

   1. Remove mop heads from handles

   2. Shake mop heads, dusters or dustcloths to remove as much dirt as possible

Doing the job:

   1. Wash mop heads, dusters or dustcloths clean in a solution of one tablespoon of trisodium phosphate to one gallon of water by working them vigorously with plumber's friend or broom handle.

   2. Rinse thoroughly in clear, lukewarm water, wring them as dry as possible with wringer or squeezer.

   3. Hang them up to dry where there is good air circulation.

   4. When dry, comb yarn out with palmetto brush.

   5. Mop heads, dusters or dustcloths, when dry, should be light grey in color, light, and fluffy. There should be no soggy or matted yarn.

Care of equipment:

   1. Clean all equipment thoroughly.

   2. Return all supplies and equipment to their proper storage places.

C. PROPER HANDLING OF SWEEPING MOPS

Handling a sweeping mop for office sweeping:

   1. Start mop at foot farthest from pushing hand, mop in circular motion, keeping dirt ahead of mop.

     a. Do not lift mop from floor or it will drop dirt gathered.

     b. Do not bear down on mop.

     c. Stand erect to prevent undue fatigue.

2. Sweep out corners as you come to them.
3. Shake mop in dustbox. Hold mop in box while shaking but do not allow mop to contact dirt in bottom of box.

Handling mops for continuous push method:

1. Straight sweeping mop: Push mop as you walk. Do not lift mop from floor. Shake mop into dustbox.
2. V-type sweeping mop: Push forward from comfortable position between handles. Do not lift mop from floor. Shake mop out at place where dirt is to be picked up.

Temporary adaptions may be needed to repel vandalism. Front windows are uncovered, but windows exposed on the rear of the building are covered during non-swimming months.

D. SWEEPING AN OFFICE WITH A SWEEPING MOP

Equipment needed:

1. Eighteen-inch sweeping mop or V-type mop.
2. Radiator brush, counter brush.
3. Dustbox, dustpan.
4. Waste paper container.
5. Putty knife.

Materials needed: None.

Before Sweeping:

1. Place all equipment in hall near office door.
2. Pick up paper and large litter from floor and place in waste basket. Empty pencil sharpener receptacles in waste baskets and replace them.
3. Empty waste baskets into noncombustible waste paper container.
4. Clean radiators with radiator brush.
5. Place sweeping mop, dustbox, dustpan, and counter brush in convenient location near center of room. Place dustbox, dustpan, and counter brush in center of room, in line with door.

Doing the job:

1. Mop-sweep floor as described in paragraph **C.**
2. As turns are made around room, shake dirt into dustbox. (If V-type mop is used, shake into pile near dustbox.)
3. Remove with putty knife all gum or dirt sticking to floor.
4. Gather sweepings into dustpan with counter brush and empty into dustbox.
5. Collect sweeping tools.
6. There should be no litter on floor, behind radiators or in corners and room should have a well-kept appearance.

Before leaving room:

Replace all furniture, waste baskets, etc., turn off lights, and close doors and windows.

E. SWEEPING A CORRIDOR WITH SWEEPING MOP USING CONTINUOUS PUSH METHOD

Equipment needed:

1. 27-inch or 36-inch sweeping mop or V-type mop.
2. Radiator brush and counter brush.
3. Dustbox and dustpan.
4. Putty knife.

Materials needed: None

Before Sweeping:

1. Place dustbox and tools at convenient place for shaking sweeping mop.
2. Brush radiators clean with radiator brush, and use counter brush to sweep under radiator or other space impossible to reach with sweeping mop.

Doing the job:

1. Begin along one side and sweep length of corridor, turn at end sweeping corner and along sides (see Figure 1).
2. At starting point, shake mop into dustbox (if V-type mop is used, shake into a pile beside box).
3. Continue sweeping in pattern shown in illustration until operation is completed.
4. Gather sweeping pile into dustpan with counter brush and empty dustpan into dustbox.
5. Remove gum or dirt sticking to floor by use of putty knife as it is reached in the course of sweeping.
6. There should be no dust streaks, dirt in corners, or where dustbox stood. There should be no dirt where sweepings were gathered with counter brush and dustpan.

Before Leaving:

Turn out lights, and close doors and windows, if necessary.

F. MOP SWEEPING A GYMNASIUM USING THE CONTINUOUS PUSH METHOD

Equipment needed:

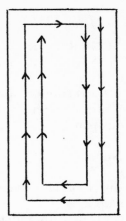

Figure 1

1. Large sweeping mop or V-type mop, and 24-inch brush broom.
2. Counter brush.
3. Dustpan and dustbox.
4. Putty knife.

Materials needed: None.

Before Sweeping:

1. Clear all gym equipment from floor.
2. Place dustbox and tools near corner opposite entrance door, at least five feet from end and ten feet from side wall (see Figure 1).

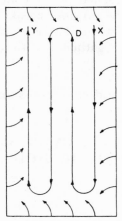

Figure 2

Doing the job:

1. Sweep dirt out from wall with bristle brush.
2. Start sweeping in corner near dustbox and follow pattern as shown in illustration.
3. Upon return to dustbox, push sweepings across to finishing point of *next* round trip. Shake dirt into dustbox and push box to point beyond finishing point of next trip.
4. Repeat process until entire floor surface is swept.
5. Remove gum and sticky dirt with a putty knife.
6. Gather sweepings into dustpan with counter brush and empty pan into dustbox.
7. Collect sweeping tools.
8. There should be no dust streaks, no dirt in corners, or where dust was gathered, or dustbox stood.

Before Leaving:

1. See that all doors and windows are closed unless instructed otherwise.
2. Remove all waste and rubbish from interior of building.
3. Turn out lights.

G. SWEEPING AN OFFICE WITH A FLOOR BRUSH

Equipment needed:

1. 18-inch floor brush with handle cut to proper length, counter, radiator, and nail brushes.
2. Dustpan and waste paper container.
3. Putty knife.

Materials needed: None.

Before Sweeping:

1. Place equipment in hall near door.
2. Pick up paper and large litter from floor and place in waste basket. Empty pencil sharpener receptacles in waste baskets and replace them.
3. Empty waste baskets in waste paper container.
4. Clean out radiators with radiator brush.

5. Use counter brush to sweep areas hard to reach with floor brush.

Doing the job:

1. Start at corners farthest from door.
2. Sweep so that entire floor will be swept when door is reached, keeping main body of dirt moving through main open area after sweeping from under desks and out of smaller areas.
3. With putty knife, remove gum or dirt sticking to floor as it is reached in course of sweeping.
4. Push dirt in pile near door, gather sweepings into dustpan with counter brush, and empty dustpan into dustbox.
5. The floor should have no dust streaks or dirt in corners, under radiators etc. Room should have a tidy, well-kept appearance.

Before leaving room:

1. Replace all furniture, waste baskets, etc.
2. Close windows.
3. Turn out lights.

Caring for floor brush:

1. Change handle from one side of brush to the other at least once a week.
2. Hang brush up when not in use. Insure that bristles are free to hang loosely.
3. Comb out bristles with nail brush several times each day brush is used.
4. Avoid getting brush wet or oily. If bristles should get wet, comb bristles with nail brush and hang up so bristles can dry.
5. Do not use a good bristle brush on rough concrete floor.

H. SWEEPING A CORRIDOR WITH A FLOOR BRUSH

Equipment needed:

1. Large floor brush; counter, radiator, and nail brushes.
2. Dustpan and dustbox.
3. Putty knife.

Doing the job:

1. Start sweeping at end of corridor next to wall. (See Figure 3.)

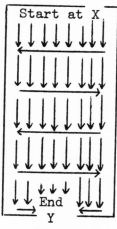

Figure 3

2. Sweep in manner indicated in illustration.
3. Gather sweepings in pile at end of corridor. Using counter brush pick up sweepings into dustpan and empty dustpan into dustbox.
4. Collect sweeping tools.
5. There should be no dust streaks, no dirt under radiators, in corners or where dirt was gathered into dustpan.

Before leaving room:

1. Close doors and windows if necessary.
2. Turn out lights.

I. SWEEPING A GYMNASIUM WITH A FLOOR BRUSH

Equipment needed:

1. Thirty-inch floor brush.
2. Dustpan and dustbox.
3. Radiator brush, counter brush, and nail brush.
4. Putty knife.

Materials needed: None.

Before Sweeping:

1. Place dustbox and tools at entrance of gymnasium (point "Y," Figure 4).
2. Clean out radiators with radiator brush.
3. Sweep hard-to-reach places with counter brush.

Doing the job:

1. Start sweeping at point "X" in illustration and sweep as indicated by arrows.

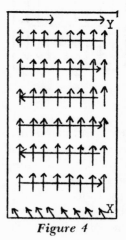

Figure 4

2. Comb floor brush bristles occasionally with nail brush.

3. With putty knife, remove gum or dirt sticking to floor.
4. Gather sweepings in pile at corner nearest entrance. With counter brush and dustpan, pick up sweepings. Empty dustpan into dustbox.
5. Collect sweeping tools.
6. When the job is complete, there should be no dust streaks. Areas under and behind radiators or other fixtures should be free from dirt.

Before leaving:

1. Close windows and doors unless instructed otherwise.
2. Turn out lights.

J. MOP SWEEPING AUDITORIUM OR THEATER HAVING FIXED SEATS

Equipment needed:

1. 18-inch sweeping mop or V-type mop, and counter brush.
2. Dustpan and dustbox.
3. Putty knife.

Materials needed: None.

Before sweeping:

1. Place dustpan and counter brush at lower end of aisle 1. (See Figure 5 "pick up dirt here.")
2. Place dustbox at point "BD" of illustration.

Doing the job:

1. Start at point "X" in illustration and sweep space back of seats, push dirt into aisles and past rear row of seats. Enter space between last two rows of section A and sweep toward aisle 2, turning seats up and sweeping under them. When aisle 2 is reached, sweep dirt past next row of seats.
2. Shake straight mop into dustbox and push box past next row of seats (if V-type mop is used, shake into a sweeping pile). Continue in same manner until aisle 4 is reached. Sweep down aisle 4 past next row of

seats, then enter between next two rows of seats in section C.

3. Repeat sweeping procedure until entire auditorium is finished.
4. Remove gum with putty knife as reached in sweeping.
5. With counter brush, pick up sweepings in front of stage.
6. When the job is complete there should be no accumulation of dirt, and corners and spaces under seats should be clean.

Before Leaving:

1. Close all doors and windows.
2. Turn out lights.

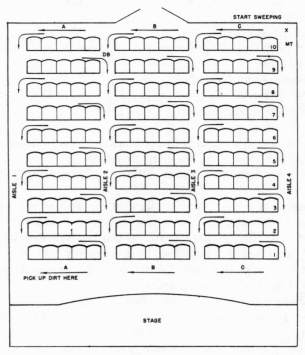

Figure 5

K. SWEEPING AN AUDITORIUM OR THEATER WITH A FLOOR BRUSH

Equipment needed:
1. 18-inch floor brush.
2. Dustpan and dustbox.
3. Counter brush, radiator and nail brushes.
4. Putty knife.

Materials needed: None.

Before sweeping:
1. Place dustpan, dustbox, and tools at lower end of aisle as indicated where illustration is labeled "pick up dirt here."
2. Brush dust from radiators.

Doing the job:
1. Follow steps and Figure 5, but do not shake the brush into the dustbox.
2. When the job is complete the room should be clean throughout; there should be no accumulations of dirt behind legs of seats, or in corners.

Before leaving:
Close all doors and windows unless instructed otherwise.

L. SWEEPING A STAIRWAY

Equipment needed:
1. 18-inch sweeping brush and counter brush.
2. Dustpan and dustbox.
3. Putty knife.
4. Dustcloth.

Materials needed: None.

Before sweeping:
Place dustpan, counter brush, and dustbox at foot of stairs; go to landing at top of stairs.

Doing the job:
1. Brush dust from radiators.
2. Start sweeping top landing and sweep all stairs and landings down to bottom landing, taking care to remove all dirt from corners of stair treads. Use putty

knife to remove gum, etc. Dust rail, balusters and dado as sweeping proceeds.

3. Gather sweepings into dustpan with counter brush and empty pan into dustbox.
4. When the job is completed, the stair should have no dust marks, no dirt in corners, and rail, balusters, and dado should be free from dust.
5. Return equipment to storage.

M. MOPPING UNWAXED WOOD, LINOLEUM, RUBBER, VINYL, OR ASPHALT TILE FLOORS

Equipment needed:
1. Two mops.
2. Two mop buckets with wringers, or a two-tank mop truck.
3. Putty knife.
4. Dry cloth.

Materials needed:
1. Warm water.
2. All-purpose synthetic detergent.

Before mopping:
1. Have floor swept thoroughly.
2. Fill buckets or tanks with warm water, adding ½ to ¾ cup of all-purpose synthetic detergent to each three gallons of water (depending on the amount of dirt to be removed) in pail or tank.
3. Stir solution thoroughly.
4. Place mops and buckets about 15 feet from corner or end of room farthest from entrance; wet floor where buckets will stand to prevent rings; keep mops in buckets when not in use.

Doing the job:
1. Take mop from solution bucket and wring it out enough so it does not drip.
2. Starting in corner, draw mop along baseboard about eight feet; return to corner and repeat action along

intersecting wall. Do not splash baseboard. If water does splash on the baseboard, remove with a dry cloth.

3. Starting in corner, swing mop in long strokes of about six to seven feet, being careful to cover all of floor. Mop should never be wet enough to leave water standing on floor. Mop wood floors parallel to grain.

4. Step back as mopping proceeds.

5. Wet mop as required. Always wring mop to prevent dripping.

6. When an area seven to eight feet square has been mopped, rinse the area using the other mop in same manner as described in steps 2 to 5.

7. Rinse mop, and wring out as much water as possible.

8. Dry mop area as described in steps 2 to 5.

9. Move buckets and mops down floor about eight feet, and mop another area about eight feet square.

10. Repeat process until entire floor is mopped.

11. Change mop and rinse water when they become too dirty for effective cleaning.

12. Use putty knife to remove gum.

13. Pick up any strings dropped by mops.

14. A properly mopped floor should have an evenly cleaned surface; baseboards should not have been splashed; there should be no water left standing on floor, and water should not have been allowed to seep under baseboards.

Before leaving:

Close all doors and windows. Turn out lights.

Care of equipment:

1. Rinse out both mops in clear water; wring them out as dry as possible; hang mops up to dry.

2. Clean mop buckets or mop trucks.

3. Return all supplies and equipment to proper storage space.

N. MOPPING TERRAZZO, MOSAIC TILE, CERAMIC TILE, SLATE OR MARBLE FLOORS

Equipment needed:
1. Two cotton or linen slasher mops.
2. Two mop buckets with wringers or a two-tank mop truck.
3. Floor squeegee.
4. Putty knife.

Ample entrance walks to a recreation center cut down on damaged landscaping and lawns.

Materials needed:
1. Warm water.
2. All-purpose synthetic detergent.

Before mopping:

1. Follow instructions for "before mopping" of paragraph "M," except reduce the amount of detergent to a minimum that will do the job.
2. Use squeegee to remove soap solution from floor, starting near corner and moving toward mop pails or truck.
3. If squeegee and pickup pan are not available, rinse soap solution mop; wring out as dry as possible and pick up soap solution on floor.
4. Use rinse mop to rinse entire area covered as in steps 2 to 5 of "doing the job," paragraph "M."
5. Dry mop area with rinse mop as described in steps 2 to 5 of "doing the job," paragraph "M."
6. Follow steps 9 to 14 of "doing the job," paragraph "M."

Before leaving:

Close all doors and windows unless otherwise instructed, and turn out lights.

Care of equipment:

1. Rinse out mops in clear water; wring them as dry as possible; hang them up to dry.
2. Clean mop buckets or mop truck.
3. Return supplies, and equipment to storage.

NOTE: If floor area is large, time can be saved by having two men do the job. One man can apply the soap solution, the other use the squeegee and pickup pan, and change water when it becomes dirty. If no squeegee and pickup pan are available, the second man should rinse and dry mop.

O. DAMP MOPPING A WAXED FLOOR

Equipment needed:

1. Two clean mops. (If mops have been used previously with soapy water, rinse mops carefully in warm water.)

2. Two mop buckets with wringers, or two-tank mop truck.
3. Putty knife.
4. Dry cloth.

Materials needed:

Clear water, and all-purpose synthetic detergent.

Before mopping:

1. Thoroughly sweep floor.
2. Mix small amount of detergent in water, if required, to remove soil.
3. Place mop bucket or truck about eight feet from wall or corner farthest from entrance to room.

Doing the job:

1. Take mop from bucket or tank and wring to prevent dripping.
2. Follow steps 2 to 10 in "doing the job," paragraph "M."
3. A properly damp-mopped floor should dry within a few minutes; there should be no damp spots, surface should be evenly cleaned, and any water splashed on baseboards or furnishings of room should have been removed.

Before leaving:

Close all doors and windows and turn out lights.

Care of equipment:

1. Rinse out mop; wring out as dry as possible; hang it up to dry.
2. Clean mop bucket or truck.
3. Return all supplies and equipment to storage.

P. MOPPING AN OFFICE FLOOR

If floor is unwaxed wood, rubber, vinyl, mastipave, asphalt tile, or linoleum, follow instructions in paragraph "M." If floor is waxed, follow instructions in paragraph "O." If floor is terrazzo, mosaic tile, ceramic tile, slate, or marble, follow instructions in paragraph "N." In addition, do the following:

Before mopping: When sweeping, place movable furniture and fixtures on an area near the door and opposite end where mopping is to start.

Doing the job:

1. Mop as much open area as possible; move heavy desks and tables only enough to mop spot where legs stand.
2. Return movable furniture and fixtures to mopped area and finish mopping room.
3. Clean floor under radiators and other hard-to-reach area and finish mopping room.
4. When the job is complete, the floor should be uniformly clean; there should be no splashes on baseboards or furniture; water should not have been allowed to seep under baseboards, filing cabinets, or other fixed furniture, and no mop strings left on floor.

Before leaving:

1. Return all furniture and fixtures to their original places.
2. If streaks result from returning furniture to original places, go over such streaks with a damp mop.
3. Close windows and doors and turn out lights.

Care of equipment:

1. Rinse, wring out, and hang mop up to dry.
2. Clean mop buckets or mop truck.
3. Return all supplies and equipment to storage.

Q. MOPPING A CORRIDOR

If floor is unwaxed wood, rubber, vinyl, mastipave, asphalt tile, or linoleum, follow directions in paragraph "M." If floor is waxed, follow instructions in paragraph "O." If floor is terrazzo, mosaic tile, ceramic tile, slate, or marble, follow directions in paragraph "N." In addition do the following:

Before mopping:
1. Thoroughly sweep floors.
2. Place mop truck or bucket about 15 feet from end of corridor where mopping is to start.

Doing the job:
1. Draw mop along wall at endge of baseboard at end of hall and 15 feet down either side. (See Figure 6.)

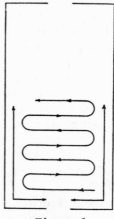

Figure 6

2. Stand in center of corridor facing wall, mop with wide strokes as shown in illustration. Do not strike wall or baseboard with mop.
3. Complete area about 15 feet long following directions for "doing the job" in paragraphs "M," "N," or "O."
4. Move pails another 15 feet down the corridor and repeat process until entire corridor is mopped.
5. When the job is complete, the corridor should be uniformly cleaned. There should be no mop strings on floor. Water should not have been allowed to splash baseboards or seep under them. There should

be no water remaining on floor.

Care of equipment:

1. Rinse out mops, wring them, and hang them up to dry.
2. Rinse out mop buckets or mop truck.
3. Return all supplies and equipment to storage.

R. MOPPING A THEATER OR AUDITORIUM

Equipment needed:

1. Two cotton or linen slasher mops.
2. Two mop buckets with wringers or squeezers, or two-tank mop truck.
3. Putty knife.
4. Dry cloth.

Materials needed:

1. Warm water.
2. All-purpose synthetic detergent.

Before mopping:

1. Thoroughly sweep floor.
2. Mix soap solution in one bucket or one tank of mop truck. Use ½ to ¾ cup all-purpose synthetic detergent to every 3 gallons of warm water depending on the degree of soil to be removed. Fill other bucket or tank with clear, warm water.
3. Place buckets or mop truck at point "MT" (See Figure 5); keep mops in buckets or tanks when not in use.

Doing the job:

1. Take mop from solution; wring out enough so it will not drip, and starting at point "X" (See Figure 5.) draw mop along floor near baseboard to a point just past aisle three.
2. Return to point "X" and draw mop along baseboard to a point opposite entrance of rows 9 and 10.
3. Face side wall from point "X" and using long, sweeping strokes, mop area behind seats to a point

beyond aisle three.

    a. Do not splash baseboards or seats.

    b. Reach as much of area underneath seats as possible.

    c. Do not leave water standing on the floor.

4. Mop down aisle three to a point near entrance between rows eight and nine.

5. Enter between rows nine and ten and mop under row ten, and as far under seats of row nine as possible.

6. Mop aisle four to point of entrance between rows eight and nine.

7. Take mop from rinse water; wring and rinse area mopped.

8. Rinse mop; wring as dry as possible and dry mop area.

9. Take mop from soap solution; wring and mop between rows eight and nine.

10. Repeat process until all of section C is mopped.

11. Place mop buckets or truck at head of aisle three and mop section B in similar manner to section C. Repeat process for section A.

12. Change soap solution and rinse water often.

13. The floor should be evenly clean; there should be no water standing on floor; no strings should be left on floor.

Before leaving:

Close doors and windows, and turn out light.

Care of equipment:

1. Rinse, wring, and hang mops to dry.

2. Rinse out buckets or tanks of mop truck.

3. Return all supplies and equipment to storage.

S. MOPPING STAIRS

Equipment needed:

1. Two cotton or linen slasher mops.

2. Two mop buckets with wringers or squeezers, or a two-tank mop truck.
3. Putty knife.
4. Dry cloth.

Materials needed:

1. Warm water.
2. All-purpose synthetic detergent.

Before mopping:

1. Thoroughly sweep steps and landings.
2. Put warm water in buckets or tanks (use only enough to do the job). Add detergent in proportion of ½ to ¾ cup detergent per 3 gallons of water depending on degree of soil. Mix thoroughly.
3. Place mop buckets or mop truck at foot of stairs in such a way that it will not be a hazard.

Doing the job:

1. Take mop from solution bucket or tank; wring out so it will not drip.
2. Mop top landing and stairs and landings down to bottom landing. Use mop strands in the hand to remove dirt from stair corners, and to remove stubborn spots.
3. Rinse mop in solution; wring out as dry as possible and repeating step (2) pick up as much solution as possible.
4. Take rinse mop; wring out so it will not drip, and rinse stairs.
5. If stair has balusters, take end of mop in hand and clean around uprights and newel.
6. When the job is completed, stairs should be evenly clean; there should be no water standing on floor. No water should have seeped between step and riser. There should be no mop strings left on floor. Stair corners, dadoes, and balusters should be clean.

Care of equipment:

1. Rinse, wring, and hang mops out to dry.

2. Rinse out mop buckets or mop truck.
3. Return all supplies and equipment to storage.

T. DRY CLEANING WOOD FLOORS

This procedure is not recommended for pine or fir floors which have not been sealed, or for splintered floors.

Equipment needed:

1. Cylinder-type floor machine equipped with 16-inch steel-wool cylinder (no. 1 steel wool) with vacuum cleaner attachment and wax bar.
2. Wax applicator if wax bar is not used.
3. Shallow pan for liquid wax.
4. Fiber push broom.

Materials needed:

Water emulsion wax if wax bar is not used.

Preparing machine:

1. Attach steel-wool cylinder to machine, making certain that key in cylinder fits in keyway.
2. If wax bar is to be used, insert wax bar in machine and attach hood extension. See that all attaching nuts are tight.
3. Set lever at base of handle to buffing position.
4. Arrange belts for low speed, that is, small pulley on drive motor to large pulley on drum.
5. See that switch is in "off" position and plug cord into nearest convenient outlet.

Before dry cleaning:

1. Sweep floor carefully.
2. Use putty knife to remove any gum or other substance stuck to flor.

Doing the job:

1. If wax bar attachment is not used, pour one inch water emulsion wax in shallow pan.
2. Dip applicator lightly in pan, wipe off surplus on sides, and apply wax evenly and thinly as possible to entire floor to be cleaned.

3. If wax bar is used, omit steps (1) and (2).
4. Push down on handle to raise cylinder from floor and turn switch "on" on handle.
5. Start buffing at one corner of floor and make long, straight runs with the grain of the wood, at speed that will clean floor adequately and allow vacuum to pick up soil and steel-wool splinters.
6. Lift cylinder gradually when end of run is reached, return to starting point, overlapping previous work about two inches.
7. Repeat above steps until entire floor is cleaned.
   a. Avoid letting machine run in one place for any length of time.
   b. Do not overload motor by applying heavy pressure on cylinder.
8. If a still higher luster is required, replace steel-wool cylinder with tampico brush cylinder and buff entire floor. Floor may also be buffed with disk-type machine using tampico brush. (See paragraph "V.")
9. Floor should be uniformly cleaned, waxed, and polished. No steel-wool splinters should be left on floor.

Care of equipment:
1. Empty vacuum bag into a metal receptacle with a tight-fitting lid. Steel wool, wax, and dirt combine to form a highly combustible mixture. Contents of bag and sweeping should be disposed of immediately to prevent fire hazards.
2. Turn vacuum bag inside out, clean it thoroughly, and hang it up (inside out) where there is good circulation of air.
3. When cool, clean machine thoroughly; wind cord carefully on hooks provided.
4. Remove lambskin from applicator, wash in luke-warm water, rinse carefully in clear water, lay out to dry.

5. Return all supplies and equipment to storage.

U. DRY MAINTENANCE OF ASPHALT TILE AND OTHER RESILIENT FLOORS

These procedures may be used for periodic and daily cleaning and buffing (between rewaxing) of asphalt tile and other resilient floors. Because mopping is not required, except before rewaxing, water damage to the floors is minimized.

Equipment needed for dry cleaning:

1. Cylinder-type floor machine with vacuum attachment, and without wax bar.
2. No. 0 steel-wool cylinder.

Before doing the job, sweep floor thoroughly with brush broom or untreated sweeping mop, using putty knife to remove any gum or other substance.

Doing the job:

1. With steel-wool cylinder attached to machine, follow steps 4 through 7 under "doing the job," paragraph "T" above. "Runs with the grain," step 5 is not applicable. However, long straight runs should be used if practicable.
2. After completion dirt and soil should be removed, and no dust or steel-wool splinters should be left on the floor.

To remove light soil from waxed or unwaxed and polish waxed floors, use the machine with a tampico brush attached. Application of water-emulsion wax for initial waxing gives better results than using bar wax with the machine. However, good results in touch-up waxing and polishing previously waxed floors can be combined with cleaning by using the wax bar.

V. OPERATING DISK-TYPE BUFFING MACHINE

Equipment needed:

1. Electric buffing machine, disk-type.

2. Tampico (light colored) polishing brush.
3. Lambswool pad—to be used only where a high luster is required.

Materials needed: None.

Before buffing:

1. Make sure wax is thoroughly dry.
2. Turn machine on side and attach brush. Tighten securely.
3. Before plugging cord into outlet, make sure switch is in "off" position. Machine plugged in with switch on may whirl handle around, causing damage to machine, personnel, or to furnishings in room.

Doing the job:

1. Move machine on its wheels to starting point, raise wheels, grasp handle with both hands, hold machine level, and turn switch to "on" position.
2. To move machine to right, raise handle slightly.
3. To move machine to left, lower handle slightly.
4. With brush flat on floor and handle in neutral position, machine remains in one position.
5. To go forward, put slight pressure on left handle; to go backwards, put slight pressure on right handle.
6. Practice in open part of room until control is mastered.
7. Always hold handle securely while machine is in operation.
8. Buff in uniform arcs at even speed.
9. Area should have uniform sheen. Lambswool pad will remove swirl marks and produce a high luster.

Care of equipment:

1. Turn machine on side and remove brush. (Remove brush when machine is not in use.)
2. Turn wheels down, wind cord loosely on hooks provided.
3. Wipe machine clean with cloth.
4. Return machine to storage place and hang brush on nail.

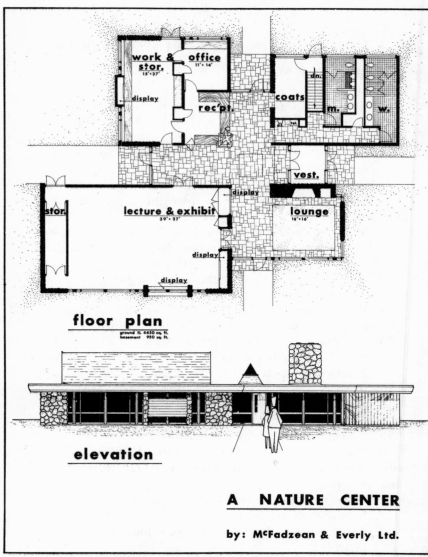

floor plan

ground fl. 4450 sq. ft.
basement 950 sq. ft.

work & stor.
15'x27'

office
11'x14'

display

rec'pt.

coats

dn.

m.

w.

vest.

stor.

lecture & exhibit
39'x27'

display

display

display

lounge
18'x16'

elevation

A NATURE CENTER

by: McFadzean & Everly Ltd.

Although the program of this recreation center is devoted to environment and ecology, operational and maintenance problems are similar to any recreation center.

W. STRIPPING WAX FROM ASPHALT, RUBBER, LINOLEUM, MASTIPAVE, AND VINYL FLOOR COVERINGS

Equipment needed:
1. Two clean mops.
2. Two mop-buckets with wringers, or two-tank mop truck.

Materials needed:
1. Warm water.
2. Wax remover.

Before doing the job:
1. Fill buckets or tanks about ⅔ full with warm water and add wax remover according to manufacturer's instructions and mix thoroughly.
2. Have floor swept well.
3. Place equipment about 15 feet from corner or end of room farthest from entrance; wet floor where buckets or tanks will stand to prevent marking. Keep mops in buckets or tanks when not in use.

Follow steps under "doing the job" in paragraph "M" for applying stripping solution and mop rinsing. Allow solution ample time to remove wax before rinsing. If the floor is extremely dirty or has several layers of wax, use of a disk-type floor machine with a palmetto brush or steel-wool pad may be necessary to loosen dirt and wax.

After wax has been stripped from the floor, the floor should be clean, uniform in appearance, and free of streaks and standing water.

X. APPLYING WATER EMULSION WAX

Equipment needed:
1. Shallow pan.
2. Lambswool applicator.
      OR
1. Clean mop.
2. Mop bucket with wringer or squeezer.

Materials needed:

Water emulsion wax.

Before waxing:

1. Floor should be thoroughly mopped and dry.
2. Pan should be clean.
3. Mop should be rinsed carefully to remove any traces of soap.

Doing the job:

1. Keep wax at least 6 inches from walls, filing cases, etc. Buffing machine will carry over enough wax to protect these areas. This prevents wax from building up along edges of walls and fixtures.
2. Pour water emulsion wax to depth of ½ inch in pan, dip applicator, and wipe surplus off on rim of pan.
3. Apply wax to floor in long, straight, strokes over an area about six feet square. Apply first in one direction and then at right angles to first application to insure entire area is covered.
    a. A thin, even coat is best for safety and service.
    b. Do not rub wax during drying.
4. Continue steps 1 and 2 until entire surface to be waxed is covered.
5. If mop is used to apply wax, dip in clear, cold water and wring out as dry as possible.
6. After pouring wax in bucket, dip mop and wring it out until it is only damp.
7. Apply wax to floor in the same manner as in damp mopping.
8. Apply in areas about six feet square, in one direction and then the other. Continue until entire floor is covered.
9. Wax should be thinly and evenly applied; there should be no dry places or spots waxed excessively.

Drying Wax: See that air circulation is good and room is warm, or wax will be slow to dry.

Care of equipment:
1. Wash applicator or mop in soapy water, rinse in clear water. Hang mop up to dry or, if lambskin is used, spread lambskin out on smooth surface to dry.
2. Pour left-over wax into container.
3. Wash mop pail or pan.
4. Return all supplies and equipment to storage.

Y. BUFFING AN OPEN ROOM OR CORRIDOR
Equipment needed:
1. Disk-type electric buffing machine.
2. Tampico brush (light-colored fibers).
3. Lambswool pad if high luster is required.

Materials needed: None.

Before buffing:
Follow instructions for "before buffing" in paragraph "V."

Doing the job:
Operating directions for disk-type machine are found in paragraph "V."
1. Run machine on wheels to starting point. (Starting point will vary with location of electric outlet.)
2. Buff strip at base of wall. This will eliminate swinging machine into wall as main floor is buffed.
3. Stand at one end of room about four feet from wall, facing wall, and buff in wide arcs (about six feet).
4. As each arc is completed, step back a distance equal to disk width and continue until within six feet of opposite wall.
5. Turn, face wall, and buff remaining area.
6. Continue buffing room in strips of about six feet until entire room is buffed.

When job is completed, floor should be uniformly buffed. There should be no heavy swirl marks.

Care of equipment:
See "care of equipment," paragraph "V."

Z. WALL WASHING—HAND METHOD

Two operators are required for this work. One man should wash the lower half of wall while other washes upper half. Man washing lower half should wash an area about eight feet long and half way up wall *before* the upper half is started. The method of cleaning outlined below does a minimum of damage to painted surfaces. Stronger agents may be desirable for faster cleaning prior to painting.

Equipment needed:
1. Two 14-quart buckets per man.
2. Two large natural sponges or two large cellulose sponges per man.
3. Several large, dry, clean cloths.
4. Platform ladder or two ladders and a plank.

Materials needed:
1. All-purpose synthetic detergent.
2. Warm water.

Before washing walls:
1. Move furniture away from walls.
2. Remove pictures, shades, or other furnishings which would interfere with the operation.
3. See that walls and woodwork are thoroughly dusted (paragraphs "CC" and "DD").
4. Fill bucket about ¾ full of warm water; mix thoroughly in one bucket, ½ to ¾ cup of all-purpose synthetic detergent as required to remove dirt.
5. Put sponges in buckets and place buckets on paper (to prevent rings on floor) where work is to start.

Doing the job:
1. Take sponge from soap solution and squeeze, *do not wring*, until sponge does not drip. Wringing will tear sponge and soon destroy it.
2. Start in corner using long, straight strokes. If baseboard is painted, wash it also.

3. Continue until an area about four feet wide and halfway to ceiling is washed.

4. Take sponge from rinse water, squeeze until it does not drip, and rinse area starting from the bottom and working up. Rinse sponge often.

5. Rinse sponge in rinse water and squeeze as dry as possible. Dry area as much as possible. Use straight strokes only.

6. Repeat steps 1 through 5 until entire lower half of wall has been cleaned.

   a. Clean woodwork on windows and doors as readied in operation.

   b. Change water often.

7. When a width of about eight feet of lower wall has been washed, the second man can start washing the upper half. Set ladders at corner where washing of lower wall has been completed, placing pails on platform or plank set between two ladders. Be sure ladders and plank are safe to use.

8. Start work at point in corner where washing of lower half stopped and wash upward, using long, straight strokes. Follow same procedure as for washing lower half of wall (steps 1 through 5).

   a. Do not allow soapy water to run over on wall which has not been washed. This forms streaks that are difficult to remove.

   b. Do not allow water to run down on lower half of washed wall.

9. Move platform ladder or ladders and planks as necessary and repeat until entire wall is washed.

10. Wall should have no streaks and no smudge mark at point where cleaned upper and lower halves meet. There should be no water spilled on floors or furnishings.

Before leaving:

Unless instructed otherwise, see that all furniture, rugs,

and furnishings are replaced.

Care of equipment:

1. Rinse out sponges and buckets.
2. Return all supplies and equipment to storage.

AA. WASHING WOODWORK

Equipment needed:

1. Two 14-quart buckets.
2. Two natural or cellulose sponges.
3. Several clean, dry cloths.

Materials needed:

1. All-purpose synthetic detergent.
2. Warm water.

Before washing:

1. See that dust is removed from window sills, above doors, or any other area where it will interfere with washing.
2. Remove any shades, pictures, or other furnishings which will interfere with the work.
3. Fill buckets about ¾ full of warm water. Mix approximately ½ cup detergent in one bucket. Put sponges in buckets. Place buckets on heavy paper (to prevent water rings) near point where work is to start.

Doing the job:

1. Take sponge from soap solution, squeeze, *do not wring,* until it will not drip.
2. Start at bottom of door, door casing, or window frame and wash upward, using long, straight strokes. Do not spill water on walls or floor.
3. When lower half of door or window has been washed, take rinsing sponge and squeeze out so it will not drip. Go over entire washed area.
4. Rinse sponge, squeeze out as dry as possible, and go over washed area to pick up as much water as possible.

5. Wipe area with clean dry cloth.
6. Clean upper half of window or door following steps 1 through 5.
7. Properly washed woodwork should be uniformly clean. There should be no dirt in corners or grooves of wood moldings. There should be no spots on walls or floors from spilled solution or wet sponge.

BB. WALL WASHING—MACHINE METHOD

Equipment needed:
1. Wall washing machine.
2. Ladders and scaffolding.
3. 14-quart bucket.

Materials needed:
1. Terrycloth pads.
2. All-purpose synthetic detergent or good commercial wall cleaner, as recommended by manufacturer of machine.
3. Warm water.

Before washing:
1. Pour about a gallon of warm water in bucket.
2. Mix $\frac{1}{4}$ cup of detergent per gallon of water. If commercial cleaner is used, follow manufacturer's instructions.
3. Test cleaner on wall to be washed. Use piece of cloth dipped in solution. If too strong, dilute solution with warm water. If too weak, add more cleaner until solution cleans without removing paint or burning wall.
4. Check reading of pressure gauge on rinse tank. If there is pressure in tanks, release air.
5. Remove pump from solution tank and pour in one gallon of cleaning solution. If commercial cleaner is used and further dilution is necessary, follow manufacturer's instructions.
6. Fill rinse tank half full.

7. Close air release valve and pump between 15 and 20 pounds pressure.
8. Fold terrycloth lengthwise, then crosswise, and attach to trowels. Cover all trowels. See that cloth is stretched evenly.
9. Allow enough liquid to flow on wash and rinse cloths to dampen them thoroughly.
10. Prepare room for wall washing as described in paragraph "Z."

Doing the job:

1. Man applying washing solution holds trowel flat against wall and moves it with light pressure in long, straight, up and down strokes beginning at lower part of wall. Do not allow enough solution on pad to cause dripping.
2. As soon as man with washing solution trowel has covered an area about eight feet square, man with rinse goes over area, using long, straight, up and down strokes.
3. As soon as he has rinsed the wall, the second man then goes over the area with the drying trowel or a dry cloth.
4. When washing solution pad becomes soiled, turn, and use again. When dirty again, remove, place rinse pad on washing trowel, drying pad (if machine is so equipped) on rinse trowel, and fresh pad on drying trowel.
5. Proceed, washing wall in same manner as described in paragraph "Z." Same precautions should be taken about streaking.
   a. If there are marks on wall caused by chairs etc., wash these after wall is cleaned in order to avoid lap marks.
   b. When woodwork is reached, wash with cloth or sponge as described in paragraph "AA."
   c. When rinsing, stay within area washed with wash-

ing trowel. This tends to eliminate lap marks.

6. A properly washed wall should be uniformly clean. There should be no water on floor or fixtures. Woodwork should be clean.

Care of equipment:

1. Open air valve and release pressure from tanks.
2. Empty machine and rinse with clear water.
3. Remove pads, wash, hang to dry.
4. Drain hose, wind loosely on trowels, hang trowels on hooks on machine.
5. Wipe machine with clean, damp cloth.
6. Return all supplies and equipment to storage.

CC. HIGH DUSTING

Equipment needed:

1. Six by ten-inch treated yarn duster with five foot handle.
2. Several treated dustcloths.
3. Clean untreated cotton cloths.
4. Curved six by ten-inch treated yarn duster with six-foot handle for dusting top of pipes.
5. Eighteen-inch floor brush with long handle.
6. Safety pins.
7. Platform-type ladder
8. Counter brush.
9. Dustpan and dustbox.

Materials needed: None.

Before dusting:

1. Place ladder near entrance of room, and place small dusting tools on platform.
2. Place dustbox in convenient place.
3. Fold clean, untreated cotton cloth over bristles of floor brush and pin securely with safety pins.

Doing the job:

1. Sweep ceiling with floor brush, starting in corner, using long straight strokes. Do not rub; brush

lightly.
   a. Turn dustcloth as it becomes soiled. Replace as
      often as necessary.
   b. Do not dust when relative humidity is high, as
      this may cause streaks.
2. Sweep walls with floor brush. Start at ceiling and
   sweep with one stroke to baseboard. Observe instructions (1) a and (1) b above.
3. Climb ladder and dust woodwork lightly with
   treated yarn duster or treated dustcloth.
   a. If dust accumulation on moldings, etc., is too
      heavy to be removed by duster or cloth, use
      counter brush and dustpan first.
   b. Do not touch walls with treated dusters or treated
      dustcloths. This leaves spots difficult to remove.
4. Use curved yarn duster over pipes, and draw lightly
   along top of pipe. Follow steps 3 a and 3 b if necessary.
5. Shake dusters and dustcloths into dustbox as necessary.
6. A properly dusted area should show no smudges and
   no oil spots from treated dusters. Moldings and
   pipes should be free from dust.
Before leaving:
1. Replace all furniture and fixtures, shades, or pictures moved before dusting.
2. Close windows, turn out lights, and close door.
Care of equipment:
1. Wash and treat soiled dusters as described in paragraphs "A" and "B."
2. Return all supplies and equipment to storage.

DD. DUSTING WOODWORK—LOW DUSTING
Equipment needed:
   1. Untreated dustcloth or untreated hand duster.
   2. Putty knife.

NATURE CENTER
Prepared by : McFadzean and Everly, Limited
Winnetka, Illinois

Nature centers require more floor maintenance than normal.
Additionally, nature exhibits require special maintenance pro-
cedures.

Materials needed: None.
Doing the job:
1. Start dusting at entrance of room. Dust lightly. Dust
   surfaces of doors, door frames, window ledges or
   sills, wainscoting, baseboards, etc.
   a. Avoid touching walls with treated dusters or dust-
      cloths.
   b. If dustcloth is used, hold lightly. Do not flick
      dustcloth as this scatters dust around room.
2. Refold dustcloth as necessary to provide a clean surface as work proceeds. Change cloths as often as
   necessary.
3. Remove gum with putty knife.
4. Properly dusted woodwork should appear bright.

Dust should be removed; not scattered around room. There should be no smudge marks on walls.

Before leaving:

1. Replace furniture or other articles moved in the course of dusting.
2. Turn out lights, close doors.

Care of equipment:

1. Return dusters and dustcloths to storage places.
2. Wash soiled dusters or dustcloths.

EE. DUSTING OFFICE FURNITURE

Equipment needed:

1. Treated hand duster.
2. Treated dustcloths.

Materials needed: None.

Doing the job:

1. Apply duster or cloth lightly to surface of tables or desks, moving in long straight strokes.
   a. Do not flick duster or dustcloth over surfaces, as this only scatters the dust.
   b. If cloth is used, hold lightly to absorb dust easily.
2. Lift letter trays, books, ink stands, etc., and dust under them.
   a. Do not disturb papers left on desk.
   b. Do not dust typewriters, adding machines, or similar equipment.
3. Wipe legs, rungs, and other parts of furniture as reached in course of dusting.
4. Reverse cloth to present clean surface for dusting, and change cloth as often as necessary.
5. A properly dusted office should appear clean and orderly. There should be no dust streaks. All chair legs and rungs should be free from dust. There should be no oily areas on surfaces.

Before leaving:

1. Replace furniture or other articles moved in course

of dusting.

2. Turn off lights and close doors.

Care of equipment:

1. Return clean dusters or cloths to storage.

2. Wash dirty cloths or dusters in accordance with paragraphs "A" and "B."

FF. WASHING WINDOWS

Equipment needed:

1. Clean cloths.

2. Bucket.

3. Safety belt (if building is equipped for its use, and windows are higher than eight feet above ground or roof).

4. Sill pad.

5. Counter brush.

6. Natural or cellulose sponge and squeegee.

7. Platform ladder.

Materials needed:

Clear water (change frequently). If windows are very dirty, use a few drops of kerosene and detergent, or 1 teaspoon of trisodium phosphate per gallon of water.

Doing the job:

1. Windows equipped for safety belt:

a. Put on and adjust safety belt. (Belt should be inspected by supervisor before being used.)

b. Place sill pad on window sill, bucket on floor (not furniture) near window, wet sponge, and squeeze out so it does not drip.

c. Raise lower sash of window, hook one side of safety belt to safety hook.

d. Stand on inner sill and test security of belt and hook by pulling on the belt.

e. Step out on sill, hook other side of belt, and test again.

f. Dust surface and frame of window with counter

brush.

g. Wash upper sash glass, using long straight strokes from side to side, then up and down.

h. Dry glass with clean dry cloth.

i. Push down upper sash and wash lower sash in same manner. If upper sash cannot be pushed down, pull lower sash all the way down and wash it.

j. Raise sash, unhook *one side* of safety belt, and step into room. *Do not* unhook other side of belt until safely into room.

k. Wash inside of window, standing on sill pad or ladder.

l. Remove sill pad, close window, and wipe up any spilled water.

m. Pick up equipment and move to next window. *Never* pass from one window to another on outside of building.

2. Washing windows without use of safety belt:

a. Place pad on sill, raise lower sash, and sit on outer sill, holding legs firmly over inner sill.

b. Pull down upper sash and wash as described above.

c. Raise upper sash, pull down lower sash, and wash as much as possible.

d. Raise sash and pull self into room without releasing leglock on inner sill.

e. Stand on sill pad and wash inner side of window.

f. Push upper sash all the way down, raise lower sash enough to permit washing remainder of outer side of glass in lower sash.

g. Remove sill pad, close window, clean up any spilled water.

h. Move equipment and proceed to next window.

3. Use of squeegee on large windows:

a. Wash window as in (1) g above.

b. Start squeegee at top left-hand corner of glass and draw it horizontally toward right (from "A" to "B" in Figure 7).

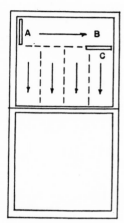

Figure 7

c. Wipe squeegee blade with clean cloth. Start at point "C" in illustration and draw squeegee to bottom of glass. Repeat until entire window is dried.
d. Use cloth to wipe up water gathered by squeegee.
e. Properly cleaned windows should be bright and without streaks. There should be no water on sill. Water should not have been allowed to run down either inside or outside wall.

Care of equipment:
1. Rinse out cloths and hang them up to dry.
2. Wipe squeegee blade and place so it will not lose its shape.
3. Return all supplies and equipment to proper storage.

Special types of windows:

In buildings equipped with casement, or pivoted type windows, cleaning of outside glass is usually done from the inside by opening window and leaning through opening. Care should be maintained to keep greater part of body within room and maintain firm grip with free hand. Exterior of fixed windows can be cleaned with the aid of a ladder if no higher than two stories from the ground or adjacent roof.

GG. CLEANING TOILETS AND URINALS

Equipment needed:

1. Small bucket.
2. Clean cloths.
3. Toilet bowl brush.
4. Rubber gloves.

Materials needed:

1. All-purpose synthetic detergent or trisodium phosphate (for deposits).
2. Warm water.

Before washing:

Place enough detergent or trisodium phosphate in about ½ gallon of warm water to make mild cleaning solution. Use trisodium phosphate for heavy soil or deposits only.

Doing the job:

1. Toilets
   a. Flush toilet.
   b. Put on rubber gloves, dampen cloth in solution and apply it to entire inner and outer surface of toilet bowl, hinge, seat, tank, and floor near toilet.
   c. Dampen cloth again and wash thoroughly under inner edge of toilet bowl. (See Figure 8.)
   d. Reach cloth down into trap as far as possible and clean thoroughly. Use toilet brush if necessary.
   e. Rinse surface with damp, clean cloth.

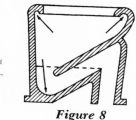

Figure 8

f. Dry outside of bowl, seat, tank with dry cloth. Flush toilet.

2. Urinals
   a. Flush urinal.
   b. Put on rubber gloves, wet cloth in cleaning solution and apply to inner and outer surface of urinal and floor near urinal. Rub harder on spots where there is any sign of stain or deposit.
   c. Rinse surface with clean damp cloth.
   d. Dry outside of fixture and metal parts with clean dry cloth.
   e. Flush urinal.
   f. Clean toilets and urinals have no unpleasant odors. Surfaces are bright. There should be no soap streaks, and metal parts should be clean and bright.

HH. CLEANING LAVATORIES
Equipment needed:
   1. Small bucket.
   2. Clean cloths.
Materials needed:
   1. All-purpose synthetic detergent or soap-grit cake.
   2. Warm water.
Before cleaning:
   1. Place enough detergent in ½ gallon of warm water to make a mild cleaning solution.

  2. Remove bars of soap, etc. from lavatory.

Doing the job:

  1. Dampen cloth in cleaning solution and go over surface of bowl and metalware, being careful to rub inside of bowl hard enough to remove any soap deposits. Do not have cloth wet enough to cause water to drip on floor or splash on wall. Use grit cake to remove heavy soil or deposits only.
  2. Rinse surface with cloth dampened in clear water.
  3. Dry bowl and metal parts with clean dry cloth.
  4. Lavatory should be clean and bright. Metalware should be clean. There should be no water or soap solution spilled on floor or splashed on wall near back of fixture.

Care of equipment:

  1. Rinse cloths and hang them up to dry.
  2. Clean bucket, return it to storage.

II. CLEANING DRINKING FOUNTAINS

Equipment needed:

  1. Small pail.
  2. Clean cloths.

Materials needed:

  1. All-purpose synthetic detergent.
  2. Warm water.

Before cleaning:

  Add enough detergent to about ½ gallon of warm water to make a mild cleaning solution.

Doing the job:

  1. Remove any litter from fountain, such as chewing gum or bits of paper.
  2. Dampen cloth in washing solution and apply it to the porcelain or china part of fountain, and to metal parts.
  3. Wring another cloth in clear water and go over surface to remove soap and dirt.

4. Use dry cloth to polish porcelain and metal parts of fountain.

5. If fountain is cabinet type, wipe sides with cloth dampened in clear water, and dry with clean dry cloth.

6. Rust spots on porcelain may be removed with soap or trisodium phosphate solution.

7. When job is completed, fountain should be completely clean. Porcelain and metalware should be bright. Water should not be splashed on wall or on floor around fountain.

Care of equipment:

1. Wash and rinse cloths, hang them up to dry.

2. Rinse bucket and return it to proper storage place.

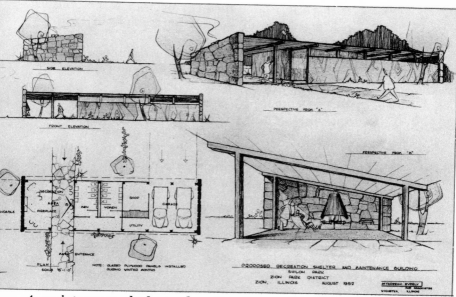

A maintenance shed can be attractive and provide service facilities.

JJ. CLEANING SOLID BRASSWARE

Equipment needed:

Clean cloths.

Materials needed:

1. Metal polish.
2. Water.
3. Two clean cloths.

Doing the job:

1. Dampen cloth with water and apply small quantity of polish to cloth.
2. Rub polish on brass to be cleaned until all tarnish is removed.
3. Allow polish to dry.
4. Rub with soft clean cloth. If any tarnish remains, repeat steps one to three and rub with cloth again.
5. If there is a large quantity of brass to be polished, rub polish on all surfaces before rubbing with dry cloth.
6. Do not spill polish on floor or fixtures, since brass polish is extremely difficult to remove from these surfaces.
7. Properly polished brass should have high luster, showing no dull patches or scratches. There should be no polish spilled on floors or fixtures.

Care of material:

1. Wash cloths and hang them up to dry.
2. Return polish to proper storage place.

KK. CLEANING LIGHT FIXTURES

Equipment needed:

1. Platform ladder.
2. Two 14-quart buckets.
3. Clean cloths.
4. Counter brush and dustpan.

Materials needed:

1. One bucket of clear water.

2. All-purpose synthetic detergent.

Before cleaning:

1. If lights are arranged so that one half of them can be turned off at a time, turn off part of them to cool before washing. If all lights operate from one switch, turn them all off. *Do not* wash any part of light fixture when lamp is lighted. To do so may result in injury or death from electrical shock.

2. Divide water between buckets. Place enough detergent in one pail for mild cleaning solution.

Doing the job:

1. Place ladder at a position convenient to reach fixture; put bucket on platform. Before use, be sure ladder is in good condition and has nonslip feet.

2. Unhook bowl from fixture.

3. If parts are very dusty, brush them with counter brush into dustpan.

4. Wipe metal parts with damp cloth, dampened in cleaning solution.

5. Wipe light bulb with cloth dampened in clear water. Be sure bulb is cool or it may break when cloth is applied.

6. Dip clean cloth in clear water, wring out wet cloth until quite dry, and clean both inside and outside of bowl. Dry entire bowl with clean, dry cloth.

7. Replace bowl, check to see it is secure. Avoid tightening screws enough to break bowl.

8. Fixture and bowl should look bright and clean whether light is off or on. Bowl should hang evenly from fixture. Metal supports and other parts should be free from dust.

Care of equipment:

1. Wash cloths and hang them up to dry.

2. Wash and rinse buckets.

3. Return all supplies and equipment to storage places.

LL. CLEANING CHROMIUM AND NICKEL-PLATED WARE

Equipment needed:
1. Soft clean cloths.
2. Good grade metal polish.

Materials needed:
Water.

Doing the job:
1. Cleaning nickel-plated ware:
    a. Dampen cloth and sprinkle lightly with polish.
    b. Rub polish on nickel-plated ware. Allow to dry.
    c. Rub off with clean dry cloth.
3. Cleaning chromium-plated ware:
    a. Wipe with damp cloth. Use synthetic detergent if required.
    b. When dry, rub with soft dry cloth. *Do not* use polish on chromium-plated ware; it does not tarnish, and the plating is so thin that polish soon removes it, leaving an unsightly fixture.
    c. Properly cleaned fixtures should be without soil and bright. No polish should be left on fixtures or floor.

Care of equipment:
1. Wash cloths and hang them up to dry.
2. Return polish to proper storage space.

MM. DAMP MOPPING CONDUCTIVE FLOORS

Equipment needed:
1. Mop.
2. Mop bucket with wringer or squeezer or mop truck.

Materials needed:
Clear water.

Before mopping:
1. Be sure mop contains no traces of soap or wax. Soap or wax reduces conductivity of the floor.
2. Thoroughly sweep floor.

3. Facing wall opposite entrance, move mop in wide strokes from side to side. Do not strike baseboards or furniture. Move back as mopping progresses.
4. Continue in this manner until entire floor is damp mopped.
5. Change mop water frequently. Rinse mop frequently. Be sure mop is as dry as possible before applying to floor as too much water will lower or destroy the conductivity of the floor.
6. A properly mopped floor should dry almost immediately. There should be no water standing on floor. There should be no streaks on floor. Any mop strings dropped during operation should be removed.

Before leaving:
1. Close doors and windows.
2. Turn out lights.

Care of equipment:
1. Clean all equipment thoroughly.
2. Hang mop up to dry.
3. Return mop bucket or truck to proper storage space.

APPENDIX: FORMS

SAMPLE MEMBERSHIP CARD

MEMBERSHIP CARD
1972–1973

_____ Center Membership

Name _____ Grade _____

Address _____

Age _____ School _____

Parents Name _____

Home Phone _____

No.

(Actual Size—2½" x 3¾")

SAMPLE ROLODEX FILE CARD

Please Print!	No.
Person's Name (Please Print)	Person's Signature (Please Write)
Address	Phone
Age Sex Date of Birth	School Attended
Parent's Name	Today's Date
Name of Person to be contacted in case of emergency, etc.	

(Actual Size — 3″ x 5″)

SAMPLE EJECTION SLIP

EJECTION SLIP

Name _____

Address _____ Phone _____

Parents/Guardians Name _____

Reason for Ejection from Facility _____

_____

Name of Facility _____

Date of Ejection _____

Period of Ejection: from _____

                              to _____

_____

Signature of Director/Manager or Assistant

(Actual Size — 3½″ x 5½″)

SAMPLE LONG DISTANCE CALL RECORD

LONG DISTANCE CALL RECORD

FROM:
Place _____ Phone Number _____
Person _____ Date _____
Authorized by _____

TO:
Place _____ Phone Number _____
Person _____ Collect   Accepted
Address
Operator _____ Filing Time _____
Minutes _____ Charge _____

THE PAYMENT OF YOUR CALL WILL REQUIRE
THAT THIS .... etc.

I certify that the long-distance call .... etc.
Signature _____

(Actual Size — 5½″ x 8½″)

SAMPLE REQUEST FOR PURCHASE

REQUEST FOR PURCHASE

Date _____   Center _____

Quantity	Article	Source	Purpose	Cost	Revenue

Approved by _____ Date _____

(Actual Size — 5½″ x 8½″)

SAMPLE TIME CARD

SEMI-MONTHLY TIME REPORT
APPROPRIATION

No. _____

Name _____

Title _____

Half Month of _____ 19 _____

Date	Hours	Remarks
1-16		
2-17		
etc.		

	Time	Rate	Gross	Debt	Net
Total					

certified correct

_____
(signature)

(Actual Size — 3¾″ x 8½″)

SAMPLE REQUEST FOR MAINTENANCE
OR TRANSFER

No. _____

REQUEST FOR MAINTENANCE OR TRANSFER

Facility _____

Submitted by ____ Approved by ____ Completed by____

Date _____ Date _____ Time _____

(Actual Size — 5½″ x 8½″)

SAMPLE DAILY ATTENDANCE REPORT

Center _____   For Week Ending _____

| Program | Grade School | | Junior High | | Senior High | | Adults | | | Day of Week | AM | PM |
	Boys	Girls	Boys	Girls	Boys	Girls	Men	Women	Total			

SAMPLE MEMBERSHIP LIST

Age Group	Membership Bro't. Fwd.	New Membership	Total Membership
Grade School			
Junior High			
Senior High			
Young Adults			
TOTALS			

Signature of Director _____

Assistant Director _____

Date _____

APPLICATION FOR USE OF
RECREATION FACILITIES

General Philosophy:

It is the policy of the Recreation Commission to encourage maximum use of the Recreation facilities by the Community whenever it is not needed by the Commission for recreation activities.

Administration:

The Superintendent of Recreation is authorized by the Recreation Commission to allow use of the facilities subject to the following conditions:

1. Priorities for use of facilities are established in the following order:
    a. Commission sponsored activities.
    b. Agencies or groups affiliated with the Commission.
    c. School sponsored activities or groups.
    d. Community non-profit recreation groups having open membership.
    e. Other community groups.
2. In case of damage or loss of property, the Commission will fix the amount to be paid by the using organization.
3. If personnel are required as the result of use by other agencies, user is responsible at rate fixed by the commission.
4. User is responsible for preservation of order and observation of all applicable regulations of the Commission, to include the following:
    a. Smoking allowed only in designated areas.
    b. Alcoholic beverages not permitted.
    c. Kitchenette must be cleaned.
    d. User owned equipment must be removed at close of activity.

SAMPLE APPLICATION FORM
Please Fill Out in Duplicate

Name of Agency or Organization_____

Address _____ Phone _____

Name of person representing agency_____

Is your organization open to general public? Yes_____ No_____

Does your organization require dues? Yes_____ No_____

　　If yes, amount_____

Is your organization within City Limits? Yes_____ No_____

Are you affiliated with State or National organizations?

　　Yes_____No_____

If above answer yes, name organization_____

Do you plan on charging admission? Yes_____ No_____

　　If yes, amount_____

Give day of week facility is needed_____

Give time of day facility needed_____ to_____a.m. or p.m.

Circle any of the articles listed that you will need:

　　1. Auditorium (stage)　　　4. Basketball court

　　2. Meeting room　　　　　5. Kitchen

　　3. Tables　No. needed_____　6. Chairs　No. needed_____

Which Recreation Center do you desire to use?_____
　　　　(Please write in any other facility to be used
　　　　　　such as bandshell, etc.)

Give exact date facility is to be used_____

Is this to be a recurring need? Yes_____ No_____

If so, list all dates, times and months you will need this facility

_____ _____

_____ _____

(Cont'd)

I agree to all conditions and requirements for the use of requested facility.

_____

Signature

_____

Address

_____

Phone

DO NOT FILL IN BELOW

- -

Approved by:

_____Director

_____Supervisor

_____Asst. Supt.

_____

Superintendent of Recreation

Charges (if any) $_____

Comments:_____

SAMPLE INVENTORY REPORT

Weekly Report
SOFT DRINK SALES AND INVENTORY

Center_____ Week Ending_____

A. Beginning Inventory_____bottles @ 10¢ = $_____
(Value)

Vendor	*Cases*	*Whsle. Cost*
_____	___	_____
_____	___	_____

Cost of Mdse. $_____

Plus Cost of Cooler
          Rental   _____

Less Credits   _____

AMOUNT DUE
          VENDOR   _____

B. Retail Value of Purchases (# Bottles x 10¢) = $_____

C. Total Weekly Sales $_____

Daily Sales

Mon.   _____

Tues.   _____

Wed.   _____

Thurs. _____

Fri.   _____

Sat.   _____

D. Ending Inventory_____bottles @ 10¢ = $_____

_____

Signature of Director

NOTE: 1. Ending inventory for previous week becomes be-
          ginning inventory for current week.
      2. A + B must equal C + D.
      3. Attach one copy of delivery receipts.
      4. Credit to General Fund.

SAMPLE FINANCIAL REPORT

FINANCIAL REPORT

Center_____ For Period Ending_____

MEMBERSHIP CHARGES WEEKLY REPORT

Memberships	Beginning Card Nos. Inclusive	Ending Card Nos. Inclusive	No. of Cards Sold	Sales Price	Sales Receipt	Remarks
Grade Schl. $ .50						
Junior High $1.00						
Senior High $1.00						
Young Adult $2.00						
Guest						
Replacement						

SAMPLE FINANCIAL REPORT (Cont'd)

FEES & CHARGES

Activity by Description	Rec'd. or Purchased	Total Available	Ending Inventory	Quantity Sold	Sales Price	Sales Receipt	Remarks

SAMPLE FINANCIAL REPORT (Cont'd)

CASH TURN-IN

Day of Week	Soft Drinks	Dues	Crafts	Other	Total Deposited	Remarks
Monday						
Tuesday						
Wednesday						
Thursday						
Friday						
Saturday						
Sunday						
WEEKLY TOTAL						

SAMPLE FINANCIAL REPORT (Cont'd)

OUTSTANDING BILLS WEEKLY REPORT

Purchased from: Incl. address if more than one outlet in the city	Date of Purchase	Invoice No.	Amount	Credit	Balance Due
Total Amount Due Vendors					

Signature of Director

Date

SAMPLE ATTENDANCE FORM

SPECIAL ACTIVITIES MONTHLY ATTENDANCE FORM

Activity	Week of	Week of	Week of	Week of	Week of	Total
Athletics:						
City League Basketball						
Optimist Basketball						
Creative Play						
Cultural Arts:						
Crafts						
Senior Citizens						

SAMPLE ACCIDENT REPORT FORM

PARTICIPANT'S ACCIDENT REPORT

PRINT

PRINT

(*Fill out in Duplicate*)

Name of Playground, Pool,
or Community Center _____

Date_____ Time of Accident____ ____

Name of person injured_____ Age____

Address _____ Phone _____

If minor—Parent or Guardian's name_____

Name of Parent or responsible adult present (relationship to
injured) _____

Nature of injury—Circumstances leading to accident_____
_____

What treatment was given, if any?_____

Was a doctor called?____ If so, on whose authority?____ ____

Name of doctor_____

Was person sent to hospital?____ What hospital?_____

Remarks _____
_____

Witness:

(Relative or Friend) Name_____Address_____

(By-stander) Name_____Address_____

(Staff Member) Name_____Address_____

_____

Date   Director

This report is to be made on every injury which requires first
aid treatment. Inform the Recreation Commission office by
phone as soon as possible, concerning *major* accidents which
require a doctor's service or where an ambulance is called.
IN AN EMERGENCY AND WHERE AN AMBULANCE IS NEEDED CALL
FIRE DEPARTMENT AND ASK FOR FIRST AID, OR CALL AMBULANCE
SERVICE.

(Cont'd)

PRINT   EMPLOYEE'S ACCIDENT REPORT   *PRINT*

NAME _____

          First   Middle   Last   (Age) (Sex)

ADDRESS _____

          Street and No.   City   State

Date of Accident_____

          Mo.   Day   Yr.   (Time—a.m. or p.m.)

Date disability began_____

          Mo.   Day   Yr.   (Time—a.m. or p.m.)

Length of time workman employed by this employer_____

Occupation of workman at time of accident_____

Social Security No. _____

Average weekly wage at time of accident $_____

Customary wages per hour $_____ Customary working

hours per day_____ Customary working days per week_____

Part-time or full-time worker_____

What was employee doing when the accident occurred?_____
_____

How did the accident happen?_____

Was workman hospitalized?_____ Date_____ Hospital_____

Name and address of witness to accident_____

Describe briefly and completely as possible the nature and ex-
    tent of injury and the part of the body affected_____
_____

Has employee returned to work?_____ If so, give date_____

Name and address of attending physician_____
_____

Facility _____ Date _____

Person submitting form _____
          _____

BIBLIOGRAPHY

All books listed in this Appendix can easily be purchased from the National Recreation and Park Association Book Center, 1700 Pennsylvania Avenue, N.W., Washington, D.C. 20006. NRPA Book Center will pay postage and handling charges on orders accompanied by payment. All prices subject to change.

PLANNING AND DESIGN OF RECREATION CENTERS

(932ATI) *Planning Areas and Facilities for Health, Physical Education and Recreation* by Participants in National Facilities Conference. Latest revision of this standard guide, incorporating recent planning and construction advances; includes many diagrams showing specific measurements; considers needs of the disabled and aging; emphasizes cooperative planning for efficient use of all community resources. Illus. $6.00 Paper $5.00

(922PGR) *Creative Playgrounds and Recreation Centers* by Alfred Ledermann and Alfred Trachsel. This standard work shows the latest developments in playground design, particularly in the U.S. The authors are internationally known experts not only on architecture but also on pedagogy. It is a wholly professional book combined with an abundance of illustrations with discussions of playground location, playgrounds for schools, therapeutic playgrounds for children's hospitals, recreation centers for young and old, and playground equipment that stimulates the child's creativity. Illus. $15.00

(936RP) *Recreation Areas—Their Design and Equipment* by George D. Butler. Outlines of planning principles, design suggestions, details of structure and equipment. Illus. $8.00

(937BC) *Mobile and Portable Recreation Facilities in Parks and Recreation: Current Design and Operation* by Siebolt H. Frieswyk. Noted in the interesting section on historical background, the outreach of mobile entertainment on this continent can be dated as early as 1524. This publication marks a milestone of progress. More than 100 park and recreation authorities involved in the use of this rapidly expanding area of programing cooperated in making this survey as up-to-date and complete as possible. Detailed coverage is given the definition of types of facilities, their design, construction, and personnel requirements. Photographs and illustrations of cultural, play, sports, social, nature and science and other types of units are representative on an international sampling. Includes a list of survey returns by type and location and general comments on survey results. Illus. Paper $3.50

ADMINISTRATION AND PERSONNEL

(1002BC) *Training Manual for Park and Recreation Board and Commission Members* by Robert Artz. Here is a lively handbook and guide for better working, better informed volunteers for park and recreation services. Helpful orientation and effective training assists citizens and their directors serving on boards, commissions, councils and committees, whether advisory or policy-making, in building a successful team for their community's betterment. $5.00

(1039ASP) *Leading Teen-Age Groups* by Dorothy M. Roberts. A revised, enlarged edition of "Leadership of Teen-Age Groups," updated to meet the needs of modern youth. Covers ways to form teen clubs and groups, program ideas and guides, characteristics of successful adult leaders. $3.95

(1042BC) *Developing Volunteers for Service in Recreation Programs* by Edith L. Ball. A guide for those needing volunteers and those already working with them. Includes recruiting, training, resources for recreation education, sample courses, etc. Paper $2.00

(1063BC) *Recreation for the Handicapped in the Community Setting* by National Recreation and Park Association.

Guide for community recreation departments, neighborhood centers and other agencies. Includes a brief report of a national survey conducted to determine what services for the mentally retarded and physically handicapped are being provided in the community setting. Paper $1.00

(791) *Playground Operation Manual* by Alan R. Caskey. This manual emphasizes playground operation and programming. Sections on games, crafts and storytelling include examples of the various activities, all of which have emerged as the most rewarding and successful practices on playgrounds in the Space Age. Enthusiastic involvement, says the author, is the key to your success in playground management. $4.95

(792) *Swimming Pool Operation Manual* by Alan R. Caskey. This manual emphasizes swimming pool administration and maintenance procedures. Special emphasis has been placed on water chemistry. All aspects of swimming pool operation are covered. An excellent guide for every pool administrator. Spiral $4.95

RECREATION CENTER PROGRAM

(AGBOR) *A Guide to Books on Recreation* published by the National Recreation and Park Association as a bibliography expressly for professional and volunteer recreation and park leaders. It contains titles and descriptions of over 1000 sources on (1) arts, crafts, and hobbies, (2) drama, puppetry, and storytelling, (3) games, (4) social recreation, (5) holiday activities, (6) music and dance, (7) sports and athletics, (8) nature and outing activities, and (9) related recreation and park topics. $1.00

(None) Most public libraries have books on specific recreation programs offered in recreation centers. Your use of public library facilities will save your personal expense.

(930ATI) *Equipment and Supplies for Athletics, Physical Education and Recreation.* The Athletic Institute. Practical guide for selection, purchase and maintenance. A valuable reference, designed for use as a text. $2.50

MAINTENANCE

(942ASP) *Maintenance for Camps and Other Outdoor Recreation Facilities* by Alan A. Nathans. Designed to meet the many maintenance needs of a camp and other seasonal facilities and recreation areas such as motels, seasonal hotels, amusement parks, swimming pools, and beach clubs and their contiguous area both public and private. It is a complete maintenance guide designed to increase property value, enrich programs, improve safety, decrease costs, and heighten operating efficiency. Illus. Paper $7.95

INDEX